# THIS BOOK BELONGS TO

-------------------------------------------------

-------------------------------------------------

-------------------------------------------------

# 2022 CROSSWORD PUZZLE
# BOOKS FOR ADULTS

# 2022
## CROSSWORD PUZZLES
## BOOKS FOR ADULTS MEDIUM

A Crossword is a word puzzle and word search game.

The game's goal is to fill the squar es with letters

Forming words or phrases, by solving clues which lead to the an awers,

The crossword puzzle game certainly is the

The crossword puzzle game certainly is the mind active.

Crossword puzzles are well-known game.

| 1 | 2 | 3 | 4 | | 5 | 6 | 7 | 8 |
|---|---|---|---|---|---|---|---|---|
| 9 | | | | | 10 | | | |
| 11 | | | | | 12 | | | |
| 13 | | | 14 | | | 15 | | |
| | | | 16 | | 17 | | | |
| 18 | 19 | 20 | | | | | | |
| 21 | | | | 22 | | 23 | 24 | 25 |
| 26 | | | 27 | | 28 | | | |
| 29 | | | | | 30 | | | |
| 31 | | | | | 32 | | | |

## ACROSS

**1** Attention-Deficit Hyperactive Disorder (abbr.)
**5** Mormon State
**9** Cheater
**10** First
**11** Canal
**12** Adornment
**13** Drinking aids
**15** Demise
**16** "Great Expectations" Author
**18** Rowers
**21** Affirmative
**22** Sacred poems
**26** Revolt
**28** Bowed stringed instrument
**29** Senile
**30** Women's magazine
**31** Ball player __ Aaron
**32** Thick soup

## DOWN

**1** Beers
**2** Mud
**3** What a bald man is missing
**4** Fears
**5** Vase
**6** Wavy character
**7** Forcefully
**8** President Rutherford B.
**10** Sign of the zodiac
**14** Nun's headwear
**17** Rogues
**18** Ms. Winfrey
**19** Playing field
**20** Redbreasted bird
**23** Swing
**24** Weight unit
**25** Killed
**27** Moose relative

**ACROSS**

1 Attention-Deficit Hyperactive Disorder (abbr.)
5 Mormon State
9 Cheater
10 First
11 Canal
12 Adornment
13 Drinking aids
15 Demise
16 "Great Expectations" Author
18 Rowers
21 Affirmative
22 Sacred poems
26 Revolt
28 Bowed stringed instrument
29 Senile
30 Women's magazine
31 Ball player __ Aaron
32 Thick soup

**DOWN**

1 Beers
2 Mud
3 What a bald man is missing
4 Fears
5 Vase
6 Wavy character
7 Forcefully
8 President Rutherford B.
10 Sign of the zodiac
14 Nun's headwear
17 Rogues
18 Ms. Winfrey
19 Playing field
20 Redbreasted bird
23 Swing
24 Weight unit
25 Killed
27 Moose relative

## ACROSS

**1** Tides
**5** Seed
**9** Horse's walking sound
**10** Green skinned pear
**11** Stockings
**12** Worn out
**13** Preoccupy
**15** Central daylight time
**16** Chester's cheese snack
**18** Apical
**21** Snacked
**22** Refuge
**26** Ranker
**28** Get from the earth
**29** Story lines
**30** Except
**31** In __ (together)
**32** Memo

## DOWN

**1** Reverberate
**2** Blot
**3** Employer
**4** Address
**5** Gross national product (abbr.)
**6** Get out
**7** Musical piece
**8** Mongrels
**10** Evaluate for taxation
**14** Trims wool
**17** Earlier form of a word
**18** Angel's instruments
**19** Pope's country
**20** Mount (2 wds.)
**23** Type of car
**24** Piece
**25** Dole out
**27** And so forth

**ACROSS**

1 Scent
5 High fidelity sound system
9 Dada
10 Removed the bones
11 Decorative needle case
12 ___ Matisse, painter
13 National capital
15 Self
16 Acting
18 Pontiac car type (2 wds.)
21 Owned
22 Perplexity
26 City
28 Chow
29 Singer Paul
30 Assess
31 Tryout
32 Looked

**DOWN**

1 Ajar
2 Input
3 Musical composition
4 Dried grape
5 Garden tool
6 Central
7 British princess
8 Expression
10 Asian country
14 Of the Andes
17 Emigrant
18 Bogy
19 Synthetic fabric
20 20th century black and white photographer
23 Shade of black
24 Deaden
25 Bedroom furniture (2 wds.)
27 Boiling

## ACROSS

1 Unconsciousness
5 Input
9 Desert condition
10 Spice
11 Comedian Jay
12 Grown
13 Beauty Marilyn
15 Visualize
16 Tops
18 Uneasy
21 Chick holder
22 Breakfast egg
26 Mary __ Moore
28 Attractive
29 Turn over
30 Opp. of false
31 Eye infection
32 Flay

## DOWN

1 Pacify
2 Brand of sandwich cookie
3 Minnesota (abbr.)
4 Admirer
5 Loser
6 Entertain
7 Covered with tiles
8 What you raise in poker
10 Cecum
14 Prestigious British university
17 Votes in
18 Unborn life
19 Nile's home
20 Awry
23 Skulk
24 Decorative needle case
25 Adolescent
27 Vane direction

## ACROSS

1 Tides
5 Supplication
9 Artist Chagall
10 Reek
11 Mormon State
12 Stick together
13 Member of an American Indian people
15 Downwind
16 Mid semester test
18 Cure for disease, evil, hardship
21 Gone by
22 Help
26 Lettuce & toppings
28 Russian ruler
29 Jeweled headdress
30 Women's magazine
31 Green Gables dweller
32 Look for

## DOWN

1 Flightless birds
2 Moderate
3 Muffin ingredient
4 Plan
5 School group
6 Smooth tightly twisted thread
7 Make a record of
8 BB Player Abdul Jabar
10 Card suits
14 Locust
17 Samples
18 Noodle
19 Once more
20 Mr. Ryan
23 Island
24 Discount
25 Star __
27 Is

## ACROSS

1 Habits
5 Capital of Norway
9 Region
10 Swamp
11 River sediment
12 City in Ohio
13 Egyptian paper (plr.)
15 Incorporated (abbr.)
16 Issue
18 Fine porcelain
21 Cooking fat
22 Ate like a cow
26 Small egg
28 Give
29 Gentlewoman
30 Streetcar
31 Killed
32 A few

## DOWN

1 Hornet
2 Opera solo
3 Bark
4 Half men, half goats
5 Tree
6 Asian country
7 Diving birds
8 Liquid measurement
10 Goods deliver
14 Ruby (2 wds.)
17 Makes into law
18 Ruins
19 Contend
20 Evade
23 Nix
24 Swiss-like cheese
25 Districts of ancient Attica
27 Rule

## ACROSS

1 French cook
5 Veer
9 Cast
10 Make copy of
11 East
12 Eastern religion
13 Poisonous acid
15 Accomplished
16 Hand bomb
18 Avenge
21 Boxer Muhammad
22 Show up
26 Knife
28 Shina
29 Pope's country
30 Decorative needle case
31 Glen
32 Liability

## DOWN

1 Gent
2 Stillness
3 Canal
4 Rim
5 __ Lanka
6 Singer Ronstadt
7 Refastens
8 Music used as practice
10 Mucus
14 Disagreeable
17 Lacked
18 Speedy
19 Thrill
20 Type of infection
23 Assess
24 Chow
25 Modify
27 Building addition

## ACROSS

**1** Russian ruler
**5** Grub
**9** Publicity
**10** What the Wise Men brought
**11** Beers
**12** Eagle's nest
**13** Neater
**15** Expert
**16** Obstacle
**18** Acting
**21** Utter
**22** Seasoned
**26** Shock
**28** Sled
**29** Mimicry
**30** Black
**31** Saclike structures filled with fluid or diseased matter
**32** Tryout

## DOWN

**1** Not this
**2** Monetary unit
**3** Imitated
**4** Live
**5** Sight organ
**6** Orderly arrangement
**7** Flash
**8** Filmy
**10** Spear-like fish
**14** Uncannily
**17** Good luck charm
**18** Jacob's father
**19** Kinky
**20** Kinds
**23** Hayseed
**24** Id's counterparts
**25** Nick
**27** Ornament

## ACROSS

1 Svelte
5 Grainery
9 South American country
10 Trouble
11 After awhile
12 Consolidate
13 "Only one substance" belief
15 Terminal abbr.
16 Song
18 Afghan currency
21 Conger
22 Mariner
26 Ogre
28 Eating house
29 Asian country
30 Belief
31 Tier
32 Salamander

## DOWN

1 Canned meat brand
2 Comedian Jay
3 Smooth
4 German city
5 __ Francisco
6 Crawling vines
7 Gambling game
8 Sea
10 Altruistic
14 Soft drink brand
17 B vitamin
18 Plate armor
19 Mock attack
20 Forest clearing
23 Caused
24 Not many (2 wds.)
25 Legible
27 Clip

| 1 | 2 | 3 | 4 | | | 5 | 6 | 7 | 8 |
|---|---|---|---|---|---|---|---|---|---|
| 9 | | | | | 10 | | | | |
| 11 | | | | | 12 | | | | |
| 13 | | | 14 | | | 15 | | | |
| | | | 16 | | 17 | | | | |
| 18 | 19 | 20 | | | | | | | |
| 21 | | | 22 | | | 23 | 24 | 25 | |
| 26 | | 27 | | | 28 | | | | |
| 29 | | | | | 30 | | | | |
| 31 | | | | | 32 | | | | |

## ACROSS

- **1** Russian ruler
- **5** Upper body muscles
- **9** Monied
- **10** Trouble
- **11** Attorney (abbr.)
- **12** Japanese city
- **13** Small bar
- **15** Fox hole
- **16** No luck
- **18** Tread
- **21** Wheel center
- **22** Chinese bears
- **26** Ireful
- **28** Hose
- **29** Went gently
- **30** Ancient Indian
- **31** Tiny insect
- **32** Fewer

## DOWN

- **1** Clawed sea life
- **2** Type of pasta
- **3** Deeds
- **4** "I've got __"
- **5** Old-fashioned Dads
- **6** Dodge
- **7** Soft drinks
- **8** Looks over
- **10** Ado
- **14** Knocked
- **17** Legume
- **18** Felon
- **19** Rustic
- **20** Humble
- **23** Big sand pile
- **24** What children learn
- **25** Salty water masses
- **27** Drink

## ACROSS

1 Torah table
5 Too
9 Voiced
10 Give essential information
11 Put on __
12 Pay up
13 Gas company
15 Vane direction
16 Make crude
18 Math & ___
21 Western Athletic Conference
22 Got smaller
26 Bye
28 Black
29 Hair care product brand
30 Healing plant
31 Slave
32 Dick Van __ Show

## DOWN

1 Ark
2 Canal
3 Philosopher Carl
4 NE French region
5 Is
6 Green citrus fruits
7 Weighted fishnet
8 Many times
10 Bring up
14 Roman magistrate
17 Look over the book, again
18 Trades
19 Highly trained group
20 Colder
23 Aptly
24 Recession
25 Joint
27 Pixy

## ACROSS

1 Syrian bishop
5 Baseball plate
9 Make calm
10 16 oz.
11 Rebuff
12 Small bunch of flowers
13 Painter Georgia ___
15 Monkey
16 Two of a kind
18 Dodger Tommie ___
21 Frozen water
22 Mainly
26 Move forward
28 Footwear
29 Zeal
30 Duke
31 Hurl
32 Tier

## DOWN

1 Too
2 Berth
3 Downhearted
4 Amount of light reflected from an object in space
5 Hit
6 Relating to the ear
7 Marsh bird
8 Brims
10 Feigned
14 First mentioned
17 Male singing voices
18 Light purple flower
19 Sporty car brand
20 Mails
23 Not this
24 Folk story
25 Bark
27 Have

**ACROSS**

1 Stuck up person
5 Rope fiber
9 Past times
10 Tricks
11 Earring need
12 Very tiny animal
13 Part of the foot
15 Cubic centimeter
16 Mouth moisturizer (2 wds.)
18 Calmly
21 Vase
22 Assisted
26 Treat badly
28 Small particle
29 Harder to find
30 Part of speech
31 Had known
32 Canal

**DOWN**

1 Monetary unit
2 Hour
3 Globes
4 Scarab
5 Masculine pronoun
6 Swelling
7 Gas company
8 Sacred song
10 Spotted
14 Goes with or
17 Writer's name on an article (hyph.)
18 Subatomic particle
19 Not rural
20 Make used to
23 Penniless
24 Decorative needle case
25 Citizen of Denmark
27 Tailor

## ACROSS

1 Baths
5 Gets older
9 Prayer ending
13 Hawaiian dancing
14 A Hindu's red dot
15 Sit in a car
16 Voiced
17 Take away
18 Vexation
19 Mother ___
21 Pistons home
23 Plateau
25 Skim
26 American Football Conference (abbr.)
29 Mink
31 Hurrying
34 Ghost's greeting
35 Sanction
37 No longer for sale
39 Fight
41 Airport abbr.
42 Express
43 Car
44 Lowest point
46 Compass point
47 Opp. of major

50 Leg
51 Compass point
52 Podium
54 Tiff
56 Constricts
59 UN cultural branch
63 South of the border crazy
64 Jist
66 Load
67 Tropical island
68 Deduce
69 Carry
70 Reasons
71 Obligation
72 Hurried

## DOWN

1 Small drink
2 Uncontaminated
3 Winged
4 Capital of Oregon
5 Atmosphere
6 Joyous
7 Comforts
8 Draw
9 Pyromaniac
10 Short
11 Change

12 Profit
14 Nap raiser
20 Floral leaf
22 Manta
24 Ethan that led the Green Mountain Boys
26 Father
27 Meeting
28 Raccoon-like animal
30 Entire
32 Musical tones
33 Dales
36 Dry stream bed
38 Sketched
40 Ponderous
42 Not rural
45 Adulterated
48 Canoe propeller
49 Reveled
53 Swedish citizen
55 Trials
56 Prophet who built the arc
57 Feverish
58 Scorn
60 Quit
61 Coop
62 Overdue
63 Close to the ground
65 Halloween mo.

**ACROSS**

1 Arrange
5 Nervous system
8 Far away
12 Capital of Western Samoa
13 Thailand dwellers
15 Rodents
16 Embellish
17 Black and white horse
18 Brand of powdery surface cleaner
19 Type of salad
21 Greek mathematician
23 Sumac
25 Tote
26 Computer characters
29 Pen brand
31 Kind of kitty
35 Twisted together
37 Km/h
39 Not female
40 Sticky black substance
41 Gave by will
44 Roll
45 Annoying, like a bug bite
47 Food container
48 Mr. Redford
50 Disarray
52 Twitching
54 Mediterranean island
55 Caviar
57 Cut with a saw
59 Competition limiting group
62 Pygmy
65 Central points
66 Slander
68 Little Mermaid's love
70 Skullcap
71 Sneakily
72 Orange peel
73 Raggedy Ann's friend
74 Yea
75 Meets

**DOWN**

1 Disappointed
2 Organization of Petroleum Exporting Countries
3 Costa __
4 Adopts (2 wds.)
5 Chubby child
6 Wrest
7 Father
8 Mixture
9 Pacific island nation
10 University (abbr.)
11 Tyrannosaurus
13 Tyrant
14 Paul's former name
20 Moved in fright
22 Hew
24 Two pieces
26 Loft
27 Path cut through grass
28 Approximate date
30 Cycles per second
32 Biblical tower
33 Say suddenly
34 Gossip
36 December
38 She
42 Value-added tax
43 Vaulted
46 Terrify
49 Striped digging animals
51 Drunkard
53 Humped animals
56 Snaky fish
58 Clever
59 Racoon's nickname
60 Phenol
61 Spring flower
63 Canal
64 Fork prong
65 Farm credit administration (abbr.)
67 Farewell
69 Discs

Crossword grid with numbered cells.

## ACROSS

1 Fencing sword
5 Artist Chagall
9 Not cons
13 Person
14 Expressing dislike word
15 Season
16 Cheese
17 Perfume
18 Negative (prefix)
19 Disappointments
21 Lesson reader in church
23 Alcoholic
24 Peter, for short
25 Grate
28 Fickle
31 Royalty
32 Thunderous sounds
34 Lubricates
36 Past
37 Shoshonean
38 By way of
39 Rive
41 Whoop
43 Children
44 Doctor's tool
46 Side notes
48 Tub spread
49 Type of missile
50 Type of cooking oil
53 Biology, chemistry, physics
57 Stack
58 Mature
60 Singing voice
61 Canal
62 Pluck
63 Pelt
64 Crimp
65 Polish
66 Skewer

## DOWN

1 Tides
2 Read attentively
3 Blue-pencil
4 Peeper
5 Inky
6 Famous cookies
7 Revolutions per minute
8 Swiss mountain cottages
9 Fake pill
10 Engage
11 Upon
12 Mix
14 Computer programmer
20 Entire
22 Estimated time of arrival
24 Mush up
25 Cogged wheel
26 Furors
27 Humor
28 Not glossy
29 Bruised
30 Delete
33 Expenditure
35 Talk back
40 Sagged
41 Locate
42 Speeding
43 Abducts
45 Ailing
47 Take to court
49 Stage set
50 French cook
51 Air (prefix)
52 Nab
53 Bridge
54 Clunk
55 Decorative needle case
56 Arrange
59 The other half of Jima

**9** Cupboards or pantries
**10** Indonesian island
**11** Alliance
**12** Chest bones
**14** Distaste for religion
**20** Dyke
**22** Shrill bark
**24** Sign
**25** Scotsman
**26** Admit
**27** Frat
**28** Scare
**29** Navigation system
**30** Steam room
**33** Dens
**35** Cincinnati baseball team
**40** Turkish
**41** Plays piano
**42** Constrict
**43** Myths
**45** Water
**47** Radiation dose
**49** Jewish last name
**50** Woo
**51** Teen hero
**52** Adventure story
**53** Blight
**54** Mob activity
**55** Otherwise
**56** Insightful
**59** Stamping tool

## ACROSS

**1** Bridge
**5** Unpaid
**9** Shorten (abbr.)
**13** Taboo
**14** Adios
**15** African nation
**16** Motor vehicle
**17** Dance
**18** Stain
**19** Mills
**21** Words to a song
**23** Pops
**24** Eight
**25** Salted sausage
**28** Scatters
**31** Disgust with excess
**32** Warning
**34** Surge
**36** Hoary
**37** Back to school mo.
**38** Regret
**39** It's time __ (2 wds.)
**41** Pinyon
**43** Touch down
**44** Mud (2 wds.)
**46** Playing fields
**48** What Celestial Seasonings makes
**49** Cliff
**50** Disinherit
**53** Fringy
**57** Eden dweller
**58** American state
**60** African river
**61** Roman cloaks
**62** Tendon
**63** Pill
**64** Eagerness
**65** Adolescent
**66** Stair

## DOWN

**1** Hang-up
**2** Pelt
**3** Negative (prefix)
**4** 12:00pm
**5** Aromas
**6** Licks
**7** Electroencephalograph (abbr.)
**8** Duality

**ACROSS**

1 Charts
5 Speaks
9 Loathe
13 Organization concerned with civil liberties (abbr.)
14 Ms. Winfrey
15 Scent
16 Walked
17 Japanese poem
18 Momma
19 Herb genus
21 Torts
23 Ice sheet
24 Related
25 Member of an American Indian people
28 From Stockholm
31 Compensated
32 Mythological water nymph
34 Deceased
36 Avail
37 Pounds per square inch
38 Possessive pronoun
39 Factor of ten
41 View
43 Sandwich fish
44 Skin disease
46 Property
48 Center
49 What children talk with
50 Chalk up
53 Instinctive
57 Bear or Berra
58 Fern seed
60 Rant
61 Baths
62 Midwestern state denizen
63 Aegis
64 Wear out
65 Loch __ monster
66 Fine dirt

**DOWN**

1 Science
2 Land measurement
3 Drop heavily
4 Cold medicine
5 Gap
6 Opera solo
7 Chatter
8 Hulled
9 Of Hominidae family
10 Eden dweller
11 Volume
12 Extremely long time periods
14 Buckeye State resident
20 What a nurse gives
22 Free of
24 Wait for
25 Potato
26 Artist's need
27 Relative
28 Timid boy
29 National capital
30 What a ghost does
33 Imitative
35 Cart for hauling heavy things
40 Advise
41 Elects (2 wds.)
42 Got up
43 Pointed
45 Big truck
47 Escudo
49 Italian "dollars"
50 Saclike structures filled with fluid or diseased matter
51 N.A. Indian
52 Seaweed substance
53 Oaths
54 Prego's competition
55 Car rental agency
56 For fear that
59 "Raven" author

**ACROSS**

1 Bivouac
5 Settee
9 Short-nosed dogs
13 Band instrument
14 Large eastern religion
15 A spinning toy (2 wds.)
16 Electron, for example
17 Book of maps
18 Be in a __
19 Lawyer
21 Martin (2 wds.)
23 Swear
24 Take the rind off
25 Finch
28 To serve drinks
31 Capital of Western Samoa
32 Huge
34 Not mine
36 Top
37 Snake
38 Oolong
39 Leg joint
41 Not brunette
43 Seaweed
44 Came in the door
46 In the middle
48 Inheritor
49 Mud
50 Depute
53 Pipe to water wheel
57 Modish
58 Say "hello"
60 Persia
61 Soda
62 Slow
63 Relive
64 Working implement
65 Sonata
66 Killed

**DOWN**

1 Unconsciousness
2 Adjoin
3 Debate
4 Pink ___, punch
5 Building place
6 Merely
7 Those who make the food laws (abbr.)
8 Solemn
9 Breath freshener garnish
10 Western state
11 __ girl
12 Gush out
14 Gretel's friend
20 Regret
22 Animal doc
24 Heathen
25 Mutter
26 Declare
27 Enlarge
28 Stew
29 Renowned
30 Fights
33 More able
35 Engrossed
40 Moral
41 Revive (2 wds.)
42 Delectable
43 Mousers
45 Electroencephalograph (abbr.)
47 Mr..'s wife
49 Acts
50 Account (abbr.)
51 Scat!
52 Grainery
53 South American country
54 Spoken
55 Casing
56 Had known
59 Strike sharply

**10** Persia
**11** Spoil
**12** Merely
**14** Sleek
**20** Neither's partner
**22** Seven
**24** Geometry concern
**25** Pros
**26** Parcel
**27** Military honor
**28** Ordain
**29** Advises
**30** Brushed leather
**33** Frosting
**35** Honey makers
**40** Sticks out
**41** Convent
**42** Subscriber
**43** Mary ____
**45** Meat
**47** Grain
**49** More intelligent
**50** Compass point
**51** Buckeye State
**52** Loan
**53** Adventure story
**54** Three
**55** Snaky fish
**56** Two good friends
**59** Caviar

## ACROSS

animals
**46** Wipes off
**1** Finish
**48** Zest
**5** Reverberate
**49** Paths
**9** "First in, first out"
**50** Serious
**13** Past times
**53** Dodge
**14** Young pigeon
**57** Journalist's question
**15** Take the wrinkles out
**58** Remove
**16** Prevaricator
**60** Region
**17** Mongrels
**61** Oblige
**18** Berate
**62** Radio word
**19** Chicago state
**63** Dig up the soil
**21** Uniformly
**64** Turfs
**23** Intertwine
**65** 365 days
**24** Dry
**66** Throw in the air
**25** Declare
**28** Jealous
## DOWN
**31** African country
**32** Joint
**1** Monetary unit
**34** Cadge
**2** Work
**36** Elver
**3** Spoken
**37** California (abbr.)
**4** Imperil
**38** "To the right!"
**5** Supply
**39** Spare
**6** Severs
**41** Kinder
**7** Shake
**43** Give
**8** Scout
**44** Hunt for Red forest
**9** Dalmatian (2 wds. )

## ACROSS

1 Tigers
5 Western Athletic Conferences
9 Ascend
13 Not there
14 Root beer brand (3 wds.)
15 Follow
16 Canal
17 Horse
18 Wear out
19 Reference
21 Musical compositions
23 Swine
24 Bridge
25 Assent
28 Handled
31 Oaf
32 Improve
34 Nerve fiber
36 Drink
37 Central Intelligence Agency
38 Cash with order (abr.)
39 Soviet Union
41 Bitter
43 Enthusiastic
44 Zeus (2 wds.)
46 Messenger god
48 Swampy
49 Bite
50 Shrew
53 Lifting
57 Chilled
58 Drug doers
60 Scent
61 Carbonated drink
62 Horse sound
63 Made cloth
64 Soon
65 Challenge
66 Murder

## DOWN

1 French cook
2 Air (prefix)
3 Three
4 Smoldered
5 Remains ready
6 Green Gables dweller
7 Central daylight time
8 Pounced
9 Large round room
10 Wading bird
11 Ecological communities
12 Sight organs
14 Orbit part
20 Affirmative gesture
22 Bud
24 Moses' mountain
25 Organization concerned with civil liberties (abbr.)
26 Strike
27 Thicket
28 Supernatural
29 Surpass
30 Long wooden pole
33 "The Real __"
35 Taboo
40 Muslim holy month
41 On the shore
42 Pastry
43 Praise
45 Shovel
47 Old-fashioned Fathers
49 Pig out
50 Permission to enter a foreign country
51 Computer picture button
52 Do it again
53 Inheritor
54 Teen hero
55 Star
56 Color
59 Ocean

**ACROSS**

1 Animal hands
5 Back of the neck
9 Part of a book
13 Snare
14 Seasoned rice
15 Ajar
16 Air (prefix)
17 Book holder
18 Loan
19 Professional Japanese warriors
21 Acmes
23 Fee
24 Sham
25 Revere
28 Group
31 Ribald
32 Looks over
34 Tiny body part
36 Maturity
37 Internal Revenue Service
38 Regret
39 Opp. of yeses
41 Property
43 Tied
44 Faithful
46 Bowling __
48 Reverse
49 Untied
50 Pediatrician, for example
53 Anteater
57 Leer at
58 Turn out
60 Accent mark
61 Real
62 Exert
63 Italian boy's name
64 Origination
65 Strip
66 Omelette need

**DOWN**

1 Parent groups
2 Region
3 Not cold
4 Jabbered
5 Zero
6 Brews
7 Bud
8 Deletes
9 Debate
10 Peak
11 Heredity component
12 Ceases
14 Sacred songs
20 Caviar
22 Touch affectionately
24 Perceive
25 Eagerness
26 Sego lilies' bulbs
27 Baby bird sound
28 Bog
29 Sensitive point
30 Adhesive
33 Commander of "Deep Space Nine"
35 Optical device
40 Fried lightly
41 Actress Julie
42 Covered with sticky black stuff
43 Hoist
45 Spanish "one"
47 Headed
49 Blame
50 Chewy candies
51 Giant
52 Hint
53 At sea
54 Excited
55 Part of a ladder
56 Lock partners
59 Nada

**ACROSS**

1 Cheats
5 Paul's former name
9 Madcap
13 Cheer
14 Status
15 Canal
16 Accent mark
17 Glass kitchenware
18 Reference
19 Explosive gas in mines
21 Asian nation
23 Bouquet
24 Organization concerned with civil liberties (abbr.)
25 New York borough
28 Killing
31 Fencing sword
32 Forms flower calyx
34 Ripped up
36 Extremely high frequency (abbr.)
37 Title of respect
38 Start to grow
39 Carpe __
41 Objects
43 Luge
44 Beat
46 Not very pretty
48 Few
49 Extinct bird
50 What the confederates tried to do
53 Powwowing
57 Island
58 Approximate
60 Entry
61 Package label
62 Sullen
63 Decorative needle case
64 Swiss mountains
65 Extremely long time periods
66 Jabber

**DOWN**

1 Tennis player Steffi
2 Bear or Berra
3 Pelt
4 Spire
5 Hinder
6 American Association of Retired Persons (abbr.)
7 Shoshonean
8 Pertaining to a vocabulary
9 Enlist
10 Opera solo
11 Building lot
12 Bottom
14 Cramps
20 Fawn's mom
22 Wily
24 Warning
25 Mind
26 Louse
27 Direct to someplace
28 Saw
29 Lordly
30 Hot cereal
33 Sugar-free brand
35 Whirl
40 Artifact show places
41 Souse
42 Trashy
43 Burn with little smoke
45 Modern
47 Unmatched
49 Submerges
50 Settee
51 Royalty
52 Cut into pieces
53 __ hoop (child's toy)
54 Small particle
55 Person, place or thing
56 Clench you teeth
59 Possessive pronoun

**ACROSS**

1 Dad
5 Partial
9 Father
13 Part of the eye
14 Rub clean
15 France & Germany river
16 Ooze
17 Egotism
18 Women's magazine
19 "Boat" car
21 Swift waters
23 Glean
24 Am not
25 Plants
28 Standing ___
31 Looked at a book
32 Mount (2 wds.)
34 Baby's bed
36 Visible light
37 Roman dozen
38 Past
39 Finish
41 Ties
43 Sulk
44 Self elimination
46 Diminish gradually
48 Bezel
49 Star
50 Now!
53 Pastry Homes
57 Island
58 Profession
60 Traveled by horse
61 Annoyance
62 First bird of spring
63 Vessel
64 Self-esteems
65 365 days
66 Citizen of Denmark

**DOWN**

1 Phonograph record
2 Region
3 Expired
4 Aimed
5 Rag
6 Little Mermaid's love
7 Dirt
8 Spain's peninsula
9 Not septic
10 Indonesian island
11 Hairless
12 Greek god of war
14 Hit the water
20 Headed
22 Colony insect
24 Bypass
25 Goofs
26 Foods
27 Swamp
28 Declare
29 Speak
30 African country
33 Carbon mon___
35 Present toppers
40 Pecans (2 wds.)
41 Sexist nature
42 Vocal
43 Featured
45 Central daylight time
47 First woman
49 Lowest point
50 Sit
51 Called
52 Buckeye State
53 Baby's "ball"
54 Midwestern state
55 Paradise
56 Ecological communities
59 Caviar

**10** Rolled chocolate candy brand
**11** A wager (2 wds.)
**12** Plateau
**14** Console
**20** Government agency
**22** Only
**24** Smiles
**25** Asian humped ox
**26** Misses
**27** Ticket to a performance
**28** Bypass
**29** Junk
**30** Sashay
**33** English sailor
**35** Saintly
**40** No hat
**41** Person from northernmost state
**42** Wet
**43** Head hiding bird
**45** Before (prefix)
**47** Business abbr.
**49** Say suddenly
**50** Gambling game
**51** Winged
**52** Fail
**53** Peak
**54** Lazily
**55** Sport group
**56** Gape
**59** Copy

## ACROSS

**1** Modish
**5** Grating sound
**9** Weight unit
**13** Hebrew 8th letter
**14** Reddish brown
**15** Kimono
**16** Region
**17** Bakers needs
**18** Brews
**19** Pummeled
**21** Japanese cars
**23** Opaque gem
**24** Passed
**25** Astronomical signs
**28** Nails
**31** Flightless birds
**32** Rock and Roll "King"
**34** Trigonometry
**36** Pen brand
**37** Charged particle
**38** Hubbub
**39** Western state
**41** Wrong
**43** Capital of Norway
**44** Done to connect papers

**46** Desired
**48** What waiters carry
**49** Bowed
**50** Parables
**53** Eager willingness
**57** Healing plant
**58** Destroyed
**60** Belief
**61** Los Angeles football team
**62** Impersonation
**63** Scratch
**64** Globes
**65** Following
**66** ___ book, church music

## DOWN

**1** Fellow
**2** Champion
**3** Object
**4** Small goat antelope
**5** Celebrate noisily
**6** Imitated
**7** Transgression
**8** Curates
**9** Least colorful

**ACROSS**

1 Baths
5 Boat movers
9 __ matter
13 Beeps cousin
14 Indian
15 Carol
16 Niche
17 Arrange
18 Tint
19 Khaki (2 wds.)
21 Deep-seated hostility
23 Snare
24 Alter
25 Stagger
28 A Salt
31 Look
32 Raise an objection
34 Small breads
36 Escudo
37 Nada
38 Bitsy
39 Rise (2 wds.)
41 Heatedly
43 Clique
44 Foremost
46 Grown-ups
48 Bend
49 African antelope
50 City
53 Oven goers
57 Bear or Berra
58 Start
60 Fencing sword
61 Positive
62 Goofed
63 Reference
64 Strip
65 Holler
66 Assignment

**DOWN**

1 Spank
2 Dada
3 Association (abbr.)
4 Spook
5 Atop (2 wds.)
6 Open
7 Carpet
8 B-Ball shoe
9 Against war
10 Threaten
11 List of meals
12 Brews
14 Hawaii
20 Miner's goal
22 Yield
24 Propel with oars
25 Fly
26 Fable writer
27 Happen again
28 Peacefulness
29 After bath need
30 Chosen
33 Cain's eldest son
35 Allows
40 Plays piano
41 Looks jagged
42 Tugged
43 Doubt
45 Mr..'s wife
47 Unpaid
49 Judge's hammer
50 Cheats
51 Girl's toy
52 Water (Sp.)
53 Russian Marx
54 Capital of Western Samoa
55 Meshes
56 Look for
59 Bard's before

## ACROSS

1 Preparation (abbr.)
5 Swain
9 Writer Bombeck
13 Small particle
14 Dido
15 Prophet who built the arc
16 Pelt
17 Forest god
18 South of the border crazy
19 Omelet cookers
21 Lack of emotion
23 Sonata
24 Energy
25 About
28 Dakar is capital
31 Sinks
32 Orange yellow
34 Tied
36 Maturity
37 Atmosphere
38 First woman
39 Extra
41 Tapestry
43 Region
44 Proportional
46 Boat pole operator
48 Hello!
49 Omaha
50 Lullaby composer
53 Nuances
57 Israel's son
58 "__ ho!"
60 Belief
61 City in Yemen
62 Plant
63 Gangster's girlfriend
64 Star Trek Automoton's
65 Fine dirt
66 Otherwise

## DOWN

1 Small fruit seeds
2 Castle
3 Decorative needle case
4 Risky
5 Unruly children
6 Food
7 Whichever
8 Former Soviet state
9 Widen
10 Cheer
11 Speed
12 Sailors "hey"
14 Fake
20 Licensed practical nurse
22 Before (prefix)
24 Baseball player Yogi
25 Eden dweller
26 Difficulty
27 Musical production
28 British county
29 Avoid
30 Dyke
33 Monte __
35 Approach
40 Engraving
41 Disconcerted
42 Seasoned
43 Whenever
45 Aspire
47 Shoshonean
49 Type of cat
50 Tell
51 Do it again
52 Affirm
53 Takes
54 Teen hero
55 Snaky fish
56 Sold at a discount
59 Flightless bird

The crossword grid (numbered cells).

**ACROSS**

1 South American country
5 Off-Broadway award
9 Wintry
13 Mined metals
14 Blossom
15 Howl with laughter
16 After eight
17 Tally (2 wds.)
18 Jewish scribe
19 Prisoner
21 Textured clothing
23 Connecticut (abbr.)
24 Multicolor
25 Esoteric
28 ___ supplement
31 Doe
32 Spools
34 Poisonous metal
36 Building addition
37 Status ___
38 Friday (abbr.)
39 African river
41 Canals
43 Pennsylvania (abbr.)
44 Clique
46 Progress
48 Stack
49 Back of the neck
50 Fiends
53 Food closets
57 Great
58 Make crisp
60 Belief
61 Second letter of the greek alphabet
62 Type of wood
63 Lounge
64 Bluish green
65 Tiny body part
66 Otherwise

**DOWN**

1 Lake
2 Canal
3 Engage
4 Drive (3 wds.)
5 ___ days (long ago)
6 Portend
7 Note of debt
8 Clears
9 Of an oath
10 Seep
11 Animal oil
12 Cart for hauling heavy things
14 Flag
20 Charged particle
22 Dewy
24 Fly
25 City in Yemen
26 Antiquity
27 Large stringed instrument
28 Tie in tennis
29 Direct to someplace
30 Tall tales
33 Supply
35 Eaten
40 Moral
41 Severe
42 Meager
43 Jejune
45 Elver
47 Choose
49 Whining speech
50 Financial obligation
51 Fencing sword
52 Brief autobiographical sketch
53 Satiate
54 Teen hero
55 Snaky fish
56 Sold at a discount
59 Only

**ACROSS**

1 Space administration
5 Respiratory organ
9 Bivouac
13 Opaque gem
14 Forest god
15 Cruel
16 Land mass
17 Outline
18 Taboo
19 Aloft (2 wds.)
21 Dummy
23 Sand pile
24 Scent
25 Future
28 Can ___ (plr)
31 Was
32 Sing
34 First light
36 Paddle
37 Brooch
38 Day of the wk.
39 Writer Bombeck
41 Utilize
43 Pros opposites
44 Pistol (2 wds.)
46 Sticks
48 Momma
49 Cut into pieces
50 Tortilla rollup
53 Hold for foot
57 Native ruler
58 Use a car
60 Canal
61 What a clock tells
62 Helped
63 Incline
64 6th month (Jewish calendar)
65 Opp. of yeses
66 Hole

**DOWN**

1 Prophet who built the arc
2 Niche
3 Type of boat
4 Boy who finds magic lamp
5 Huge
6 Western state
7 New York City
8 Beowulf's foe
9 Put in the middle
10 Assure
11 Short
12 Cabal
14 Closefisted
20 Barbarian
22 Charged particle
24 Starts
25 Band instrument
26 Dreads
27 Italian physicist
28 Disgrace
29 City Boca ___
30 Moved back and forth
33 Musical production
35 Loch __ monster
40 Suitor
41 Muslim holy month
42 Reverberated
43 Zeroes
45 Feed
47 Oodles
49 Inlets
50 Soft cheese from Greece
51 Among
52 The other half of Iwo
53 Bona __
54 Spoken
55 Fancy car
56 Department (abbr.)
59 River (Spanish)

**ACROSS**

1 Hook part
5 South of the border crazy
9 Opaque gem
13 Dunking cookies
14 Necklace fastener
15 ___ matter
16 Clothing stitch
17 Artery
18 Hind end
19 _____ Eggs(Easter treats)
21 Universe
23 Imitated
24 Asian nation
25 Hair ___
28 Female Performer
31 Institution (abbr.)
32 Type of race
34 Treaty organization
36 Compass point
37 Nada
38 Charged particle
39 Ecological communities
41 Renounce allegiance
43 Narrow opening
44 Giant wave
46 UN cultural branch
48 Italian boy's name
49 Cereal ingredient
50 Threads
53 Smaller than destroyer ships
57 Scent
58 Moses' brother
60 Hose
61 Bounce
62 Clank
63 Band instrument
64 Woo
65 Part of the "KKK"
66 Stink

**DOWN**

1 Pear type
2 Region
3 Looked at a book
4 Pompous language
5 Architect Frank ___ Wright
6 Boat movers
7 Clock time
8 Sate of being opaque
9 Rowers
10 Damson
11 Bullets
12 What dogs sit on
14 Calling
20 United Parcel Service
22 Paddle
24 Balancer
25 Feel the lack of
26 Beginning
27 Drug doers
28 Excuse
29 Boat locomotion needs
30 Unblinking
33 Opposite of ally
35 Upon
40 Greek muse of music
41 Rifle
42 Coaxing
43 State representative
45 Neither's partner
47 Nettle
49 Manhattan's neighbor
50 Crimp
51 Belief
52 Yacht
53 German "Mrs."
54 Brass
55 Black
56 Look for
59 Entire

**11** Memorization
**12** Elated
**14** Skewed
**20** Set of tools
**22** Vane direction
**24** Nook
**25** Paul's former name
**26** Full of life
**27** Water retention
**28** Spongy
**29** Relating to the ear
**30** South American animal
**33** Dine
**35** Had known
**40** Cleaning chemical
**41** Somethings to run
**42** Occupied lodgings
**43** Oration room environment
**45** Pan's partner
**47** Avail
**49** Famous brand of blue jeans
**50** Prod
**51** Shine
**52** Grass
**53** Beat severely
**54** Fasten
**55** Land measurement
**56** Body of water
**59** Bard's before

## ACROSS

**1** Fastener
**5** Apple type
**9** Floating ice
**13** Dunking cookies
**14** Spite
**15** Absent without leave
**16** Chair
**17** 1997 Madonna movie
**18** Sixth Greek letter
**19** Small parrot
**21** Equipped, with "up"
**23** Energy
**24** One of Columbus' ships
**25** Sleek
**28** Mica
**31** Helper
**32** Tie in tennis
**34** Brood
**36** Shoshonean
**37** Fire remains
**38** Fled
**39** Dalai __
**41** Anesthetic
**43** Identical
**44** Funnel-shaped fish
**46** Criminal
**48** AM
**49** Mislay
**50** Jai alai
**53** Benthic
**57** Asian country
**58** Sensitive point
**60** S.A. Indian
**61** Green fruit
**62** Ancient Celtic priest
**63** Revelry
**64** Volcano
**65** Compass point
**66** Fencing sword

## DOWN

**1** Hospital (abbr.)
**2** Region
**3** Scorch
**4** Drinkable
**5** High temperature
**6** Part
**7** Gained
**8** Ideate
**9** Marketplaces
**10** Vessel

11 Memorization
12 Elated
14 Skewed
20 Set of tools
22 Vane direction
24 Nook
25 Paul's former name
26 Full of life
27 Water retention
28 Spongy
29 Relating to the ear
30 South American animal
33 Dine
35 Had known
40 Cleaning chemical
41 Somethings to run
42 Occupied lodgings
43 Oration room
    environment
45 Pan's partner
47 Avail
49 Famous brand of blue
    jeans
50 Prod
51 Shine
52 Grass
53 Beat severely
54 Fasten
55 Land measurement
56 Body of water
59 Bard's before

## ACROSS

1 Fastener
5 Apple type
9 Floating ice
13 Dunking cookies
14 Spite
15 Absent without leave
16 Chair
17 1997 Madonna movie
18 Sixth Greek letter
19 Small parrot
21 Equipped, with "up"
23 Energy
24 One of Columbus' ships
25 Sleek
28 Mica
31 Helper
32 Tie in tennis
34 Brood
36 Shoshonean
37 Fire remains
38 Fled
39 Dalai __
41 Anesthetic
43 Identical
44 Funnel-shaped fish

46 Criminal
48 AM
49 Mislay
50 Jai alai
53 Benthic
57 Asian country
58 Sensitive point
60 S.A. Indian
61 Green fruit
62 Ancient Celtic priest
63 Revelry
64 Volcano
65 Compass point
66 Fencing sword

## DOWN

1 Hospital (abbr.)
2 Region
3 Scorch
4 Drinkable
5 High temperature
6 Part
7 Gained
8 Ideate
9 Marketplaces
10 Vessel

**ACROSS**

1 Association (abbr.)
5 Fable
9 Beeps cousin
13 Syllables used in songs (2 wds.)
14 Sticky
15 Small mountain
16 A spinning toy (2 wds.)
17 Peeved
18 Belief
19 Reword
21 Medicine
23 Tint
24 Boat movers
25 Prestige
28 Cannoneers
31 Gumbo
32 Composer Francis __ Key
34 Not whites
36 Ocean
37 Concealed
38 Put on
39 Hebrew 8th letter
41 Petty
43 Peter, for short
44 Group
46 Worthless
48 Pros opposites
49 Wail
50 Cured
53 Air letter
57 Supplication
58 Allegory
60 Ancien German character
61 Soviet Union
62 Uninvited
63 Teen hero
64 Love flower
65 Greek stringed instrument
66 Fix

**DOWN**

1 Far away
2 Satiate
3 Swill
4 Flammable liquid
5 Type of code
6 Join
7 Ball holder
8 Water holder
9 Wish
10 Helper
11 Luge
12 Fun
14 Very large people
20 Caviar
22 Sea eagle
24 Beat
25 Blackjack
26 BB Player Abdul Jabar
27 Shipping container
28 On your way
29 Cowboy show
30 Narrow openings
33 Lower parts of faces
35 Leg joint
40 10,000 squared meters
41 Considerate
42 Made a menacing noise
43 Puritan
45 Digit
47 Deuce
49 Negate
50 Goad
51 Ditto
52 Not as much
53 Shorten (abbr.)
54 Unrefined
55 Soon
56 Blend
59 Whichever

**ACROSS**

1 Adventure story
5 Prego's competition
9 Friend
13 Lowest in rank
14 Confuse
15 Engage
16 Persia
17 Worm-like insect stage
18 Association (abbr.)
19 Home to Denver and Boulder
21 National capital
23 Sweet potatoes
24 Totals
25 Go back on a promise
28 Constructing outside of painting
31 Native ruler
32 Sitting room
34 Broth
36 Electroencephalograph (abbr.)
37 Large vehicle
38 Tell a tall tale
39 Had known
41 Worked at
43 Vegetable
44 Bored
46 Destroyer
48 Cogged wheel
49 Opp. of loud
50 N. Western state
53 Swiveling
57 Small bottle
58 Music used as practice
60 Economics abrv.
61 Niche
62 Utters
63 Star
64 Dregs
65 Sold at a discount
66 Frozen rain

**DOWN**

1 __ and span
2 Air (prefix)
3 Destination
4 Teaser
5 Skims over a book
6 Big hairdo
7 Governor
8 Kampala resident
9 Bod
10 Snake sound
11 __ Minor (Little Dipper)
12 List of meals
14 Picks on
20 Newspaper
22 High naval rank (abbr.)
24 Woken
25 Stink
26 Improve
27 African country
28 Liquid
29 Mr. Ryan
30 Deception
33 More able
35 Look
40 Squirms
41 Worlds
42 Crowds of moving animals
43 Baby cats
45 Constellation
47 Unidentified flying object
49 Sashay
50 Egg-shaped
51 Aged
52 Relive
53 Twang
54 Computer picture button
55 De __ (from the beginning)
56 Bite
59 Oolong

**10** Economics abrv.
**11** Footgear
**12** Exam
**14** Sandwich leftovers
**20** Weapon
**22** School group
**24** Woodwind player
**25** At sea
**26** Necklace fastener
**27** Pope's governing organization
**28** Petty
**29** Understandable
**30** Music used as practice
**33** At no time
**35** Perceives with eye
**40** Difficult
**41** Physics motion tendency
**42** Juveniles
**43** "Unsinkable ship"
**45** Ball holder
**47** Roman dozen
**49** Soap operas
**50** Electrical current unit
**51** Opera solo
**52** Look
**53** Building lot
**54** Indonesian island
**55** Gait
**56** Otherwise
**59** Porker

## ACROSS

**1** Father
**5** Fly
**9** Bird's home
**13** Night light
**14** Willed
**15** Hurt
**16** Capital of Norway
**17** Corroded
**18** Hisses
**19** Skeet shooters
**21** Upright
**23** Corn's clothes
**24** House animals
**25** Emphasizing a syllable
**28** What prayers often seek
**31** Speak indistinctly
**32** Cuts
**34** Not ins
**36** Hearing part
**37** Vane direction
**38** Prompt
**39** Land mass
**41** Pearl
**43** Brand of laundry detergent
**44** Spouse
**46** Oxygen compounds
**48** Doe
**49** Lawyer dress
**50** Appraiser
**53** Possible to satisfy
**57** Dunking cookies
**58** Bird portion
**60** Nab
**61** In __ of
**62** Tiny amounts
**63** Evils
**64** Sticky black substances
**65** Gets older
**66** Reference

## DOWN

**1** Famous cookies
**2** Baloney
**3** Knife
**4** One more
**5** Clod
**6** Defeat
**7** Eastern Standard Time
**8** Fountains
**9** Triscut company

10 Old
11 Ice sheet
12 Doting
14 Loan shark
20 Rested
22 Writing liquid
24 __ Vice (tv show)
25 Chair
26 Annoys
27 Chosen
28 Cut of beef
29 Household insect
30 Japanese dish
33 Leaning
35 Former
40 Gives hard time
41 Meekest
42 Alter
43 A Salt
45 Caviar
47 Grain
49 Pool
50 Prego's competition
51 Wading bird
52 Compass point
53 Drop heavily
54 Spoken
55 Loch __ monster
56 Interest
59 Communication Workers
   of America (abr.)

## ACROSS

1 Leer at
5 Discerning
9 Strike
13 Small bird
14 Remove from the box
15 Capital of Norway
16 Star
17 Saudi Arabian citizen
18 Billions of years
19 Bikini
21 Belted
23 Royalty
24 Not women's
25 Sleek
28 Putters
31 Snaky fish
32 National capital
34 Beat
36 Wood chopper
37 Male cat
38 Fire remains
39 Technical
41 Something very small
43 Hurt
44 Oration room

environment
46 Sea __
48 Horse
49 Eye infection
50 Took a chance
53 Light, open carriages
57 Cain killed him
58 Widely known
60 Region
61 Scoff
62 Cussed
63 Assignment
64 Soviet Union
65 Record
66 Otherwise

## DOWN

1 Has
2 Expand
3 Israel's son
4 Types of paint
5 Escargot
6 Adjoin
7 Titan
8 Taxing
9 Cruder

**ACROSS**

1 Tennis player Steffi
5 Wood cutting tools
9 Part of a football player's gear
13 Fancy car
14 Excuse
15 Healing plant
16 Ended
17 Biblical food
18 Attractive
19 Recently married man
21 Unfit
23 Fredrick's nickname
24 Vassal
25 South-Central Dravidian
28 Sampling food
31 Paradise
32 Cook with fat
34 Sidewalk and road separator
36 Hubbub
37 Women's undergarment
38 Constellation
39 Lay
41 Dye
43 Open tart-like pastry
44 Discloses
46 Moral
48 Scarce
49 Take by surprise
50 Soak up
53 Jumping
57 Grainery
58 Musical production
60 Teen hero
61 Move effortlessly
62 Celebrate noisily
63 Otherwise
64 Meshes
65 Speaks
66 Was looked at

**DOWN**

1 Ball
2 Rend
3 Prayer ending
4 Come before as symbol of what is to come
5 Loose
6 Am not
7 West by north
8 Thai
9 Peaceable
10 Short for aluminum
11 Pamper
12 Origination
14 __ curiae
20 Shovel
22 Artist's creation
24 Devil
25 Tyrant
26 Bedspread feather
27 Untied
28 Sheers
29 Voids
30 Huge
33 White poplar
35 Cram
40 Dens (2 wds.)
41 Conceals feelings
42 Tangible
43 Likes
45 Hearing part
47 Barbarian
49 Aches
50 Association (abbr.)
51 Levee
52 Narrow opening
53 Large group
54 Bored
55 Pry
56 Dale
59 Pod vegetable

## ACROSS

1 Musical notation
5 Monetary unit
9 In ___ (together)
13 Ardent
14 Used a needle and thread
15 Call a cab
16 Wager
17 "The Real ___"
18 S.A. Indian
19 Baja beach
21 Desired
23 Taverns
24 Elated
25 Screech like a bird
28 Bringing together
31 Put a picture up
32 Berried shrub
34 Rotating mechanism
36 Klutz
37 South by west
38 Statute
39 Blue-pencil
41 Visitor
43 Regulation
44 Astral
46 Pressed
48 Churn
49 Traced
50 Organized massacre
53 Able to be stowed
57 Citizen
58 Shrimp
60 Berate
61 Billboard
62 Steam room
63 Expires
64 Pill
65 Whirl
66 Veer

## DOWN

1 Tyrant
2 Comedian Jay
3 Food
4 Slang for dirty hotel (2 wds.)
5 Factions
6 Young Women's Christian Association
7 Constellation
8 Picturesque
9 Shindy
10 Yin's partner
11 Pleasant
12 Robed
14 Gives a cocky grin
20 Underdone
22 Cereal
24 Chew like a rodent
25 Footgear
26 Courtyards
27 Maimed
28 Deep brown
29 Man-made fiber
30 Order
33 Normal
35 Unpaid
40 Earthenware container
41 Brief look
42 Albanian capital
43 Fearful people
45 Lavatory
47 Crimson
49 Fluffy
50 Posttraumatic stress disorder
51 Buckeye State
52 Mouth stoppers
53 Praise
54 Security
55 In ___ of
56 Otherwise
59 Radiation dose

**ACROSS**

1 False stories
5 Pros
9 Wail
13 Bored
14 What a dropped melon does
15 Region
16 Was looked at
17 Drogue
18 Prejudice
19 Informal talk
21 Kansas City baseball team
23 Ripe
24 Ceases
25 Award
28 Joining metal
31 Shaft
32 Narrative
34 Wear out
36 Accountant
37 French "yes"
38 Cow food
39 Polish
41 Sleep disorder
43 Reference
44 Hurt one's toe
46 Went out of bounds
48 Pelt
49 Snare
50 Outcome
53 "Light" cola type
57 Fly alone
58 Identicals
60 Bloc
61 Eagerness
62 Planet
63 Retain
64 Silly
65 Colors
66 Want

**DOWN**

1 State treasury
2 Belief
3 Type of cheese
4 Sense perceived
5 Louse
6 Hint
7 Feed
8 Strictly
9 Tend
10 Opera solo
11 Wale
12 Female child
14 Turns
20 Self
22 Unmatched
24 Spooky
25 German composer
26 Big exhibits
27 Slope
28 Bruise
29 Zero
30 Rub
33 What a cherry is to a sundae
35 Looked
40 Pleasant combination of sounds
41 Adjoined
42 Again
43 Little cake cooked in cup-shaped holder
45 Condemn
47 Cereal
49 Hues
50 Old
51 Field game
52 Strike
53 Desperate
54 Wagon pullers
55 Capital of the Ukraine
56 Spot
59 Behavior

**ACROSS**

1 Father
5 Duces
9 Deeds
13 Factual
14 Asian nation
15 Churn
16 Tranquilize
17 Sacred poem
18 Particular form
19 Waist toy (2 wds.)
21 Spoke
23 Lighted sign
24 Eager
25 N.J. airport
28 Swaziland capital
31 Little Mermaid's love
32 Scrub
34 Speaks
36 Start to grow
37 Owns
38 Killed in action
39 Fencing sword
41 Red and white drinks
43 Bowed
44 Hunters
46 Bind
48 Exchange
49 Mob activity
50 Alternative
53 Strict
57 Scarce
58 Adult insect
60 Ditto
61 Aegis
62 Day's opposite
63 365 days
64 September (abbr.)
65 Overeat
66 Opp. of loud

**DOWN**

1 Bend
2 Swain
3 Sphere
4 ___ Almanac (yearly
5 Chicken brand
6 Wind
7 Fat
8 Metal urn with spigot
9 Navies
10 Bird
11 Brand of laundry detergent
12 Luge
14 Ghosts
20 That woman
22 Cut of beef
24 Treat badly
25 Northeast by east
26 Burst out
27 Broader
28 Groans
29 Nude
30 Looking at
33 Twirp
35 Satiate
40 Least difficult
41 Getting off the bottle
42 Faucet
43 Misleads
45 Cash with order (abr.)
47 Lavatory
49 What you do to wrongs
50 Mined metals
51 Part of a book
52 Trigger
53 Prego's competition
54 Tub spread
55 U.S. Air Force
56 Arrange
59 Cc

## ACROSS

1 Adam's son
5 Compass point
9 Volcano
13 One time
14 Schism
15 Cry like a cat
16 Store
17 Commander of "Deep Space Nine"
18 Dada
19 Bonsai (2 wds.)
21 Capital of Niger
23 Unpaid
24 Fuzz
25 Account for safe keeping
28 Snacks
31 Leer
32 Canned chili brand
34 Yin's partner
36 Scientist's office
37 Sorbet
38 Also
39 Goofs
41 Mr. Seinfeld
43 Air (prefix)
44 1972 Winter Olympic location
46 Deserved
48 Chest bones
49 Piece
50 Old Testament prophet
53 Hoarsest
57 Organization of Petroleum Exporting Countries
58 Put on a pedestal
60 Eye infection
61 Island
62 Timid boy
63 Sandwich fish
64 Allows
65 Building lot
66 Unwell

## DOWN

1 Price
2 Negative (prefix)
3 Computer picture button
4 Original colony state (2 wds.)
5 Saw
6 Otherwise
7 Pen brand
8 Throwing rocks
9 Emotional understanding
10 Sport group
11 No
12 Out
14 Turns
20 Deuce
22 Business abbr.
24 Type of gun
25 Women's magazine
26 Flies
27 Poisonous snake
28 Opposite of micro
29 Dine
30 What people do in their sleep
33 Layers
35 Saintly
40 Tidies
41 Unemployed
42 Frothy
43 Painters and sculptors
45 Desert
47 __ of the covenant
49 Single beat
50 Taint
51 Niche
52 Become runny
53 Poetic "has"
54 Decorative needle case
55 In __ (together)
56 Wood
59 Roman dozen

## ACROSS

1 Delude
5 Audio-system
9 Data transmission rate
13 At sea
14 Small Mediterranean boat
15 Ditto
16 Doe
17 Carbon mon__
18 What children talk with
19 Left without parents
21 Campanile
23 Bloc
24 Motor vehicle
25 Inhospitable
28 Claw
31 Except
32 On your way
34 Told
36 Child
37 Wrath
38 Compass point
39 Tip
41 Childrens sliding toys
43 Discerning
44 Begins again
46 Tranquilized
48 Far away
49 Allot (with "out")
50 How do you dos
53 Flaring
57 Shine
58 Hastening
60 Entry
61 Be angry
62 Spooky
63 Decorative needle case
64 Tyrant
65 Prow
66 Jabber

## DOWN

1 Pedestal part
2 Drug doer
3 Chirping sound
4 Amelia ___
5 Curses
6 As previously cited
7 Government worker
8 Lettuce type
9 Voting means
10 First letter of the Arabic alphabet
11 Soviet Union
12 Silly
14 Defining districts
20 Wood chopper
22 Estimated time of arrival
24 Pimpled
25 Pear type
26 'love' (Italian)
27 Laundry cycle
28 Fathers
29 Irrigation ditch
30 Joint
33 Cargo vessel
35 Accomplishment
40 Contains Book of Psalms
41 Bashed
42 Sleigh
43 Svelte
45 Unidentified flying object
47 Shoshonean
49 Something very small
50 Lift
51 Flightless birds
52 National capital
53 Telegram
54 Small particle
55 Person, place or thing
56 Clench you teeth
59 Still

## Crossword Grid

**ACROSS**

1 German composer
5 Magnificence
9 Coffeehouse
13 Water (Sp.)
14 Greek philosopher
15 Baker's need
16 Reorient
17 Worm-like insect stage
18 Baron
19 Rash
21 Circus comedians
23 Canned meat brand
24 Reasons
25 Number to be added
28 Dairy product types
31 Beat
32 Relating to the sun
34 Not out of
36 Twitching
37 Doctor (slang)
38 Ocean
39 Fasten
41 Strong drink
43 Lawyer dress
44 Small aircrafts
46 Salad need
48 Pros opposites
49 Weight unit
50 Team spirit
53 Hermit like
57 Greek god of war
58 Spooky
60 Au naturel
61 Optical device
62 Controls
63 Cain killed him
64 Dorothy's dog
65 Luge
66 Factual

**DOWN**

1 Wash
2 Accent mark
3 Heal
4 Combined telephone transmitter and receiver
5 Plasma
6 Boat movers
7 I want my ___
8 Fishes illegally
9 Gigantic statues
10 Assure
11 Spore plant
12 Ceases
14 Offers as an excuse
20 Licensed practical nurse
22 Caustic substance
24 Wham
25 Branch of learning
26 Executing
27 Relating to a Duke
28 Dirt clumps
29 Turn out
30 Mug
33 Aromas
35 Grain
40 Cubist painter
41 Flitches
42 Matches
43 Lecture
45 Pain unit
47 Cram
49 Toil
50 Thick drink
51 Dunking cookies
52 Engage
53 Canal
54 Hose
55 Belief
56 Tiny body part
59 Elver

10 Weight unit
11 Usages
12 Delivered by post
14 Lifting machines
20 Bad (prefix)
22 Boxer Muhammad
24 Relish
25 __ and span
26 Record
27 Small wrapped candies
28 People who get things done
29 Utilization
30 Nigerian capital
33 Type of mob
35 Lay
40 Occupy wholly
41 Not western
42 Spring flowers
43 Omelet (2 wds.)
45 Note of debt
47 Not (refix)
49 Steps for crossing a fence
50 Security
51 Women's magazine
52 Island
53 Liner
54 Upon
55 Western state
56 It's time __ (2 wds.)
59 Also

**ACROSS**

1 Supplication
5 Dorothy's dog
9 Flightless birds
13 Engrossed
14 Head
15 Pry
16 Except
17 Check out books again
18 Dale
19 Protective face covering (2 wds.)
21 Most uncommon
23 Horse hair
24 Joyful
25 Taste
28 Obedient
31 Small ground plot
32 Splash
34 Tyrant
36 Large computer co.
37 Still
38 Maturity
39 Chop
41 Enter
43 Self-esteems

44 Madmen
46 Eat
48 Oh my __! (slang)
49 Slug
50 Capital of Lebanon
53 Excel (2 wds.)
57 Ditto
58 Moral principles
60 Not out of
61 Evils
62 Churns
63 Male deer
64 Dregs
65 No
66 Santa call (2 wds.)

**DOWN**

1 Professor (abbr.)
2 Dalai __
3 Great
4 Strive
5 Not those
6 Pit noise
7 Ball holder
8 Grapes ___ (2 wds.)
9 Implant

**ACROSS**

1 University (abbr.)
5 Prego's competition
9 Niche
13 Biblical "you"
14 Woman
15 Not cons
16 Boat movers
17 Toothbrush brand
18 SOS!
19 Advocate
21 Argue logically
23 Far away
24 Sacks
25 Favorite vacation spot
28 Pleading
31 Winged
32 Shut down
34 Lacing
36 Three
37 The other half of Jima
38 By way of
39 Animal oil
41 Dimensions
43 Dinner table seasoning
44 Doctor's tool
46 Dishevel someone's hair
48 Reverse
49 Nail
50 Where, poetically
53 Woven leather sandal
57 __ and ruin
58 Full of swamp grass
60 Colt
61 Healing plant
62 Urges
63 Goofs
64 Pennsylvania (abbr.)
65 Merely
66 Interbreeding population
   within a species

**DOWN**

1 A spinning toy (2 wds.)
2 Blacken
3 Air (prefix)
4 Loss of hope
5 Less cooked
6 6th month (Jewish
   calendar)
7 Girl
8 Offense
9 Inability to use words
10 President (abbr.)
11 Fly alone
12 Sports channel
14 Tile art
20 Often poetically
22 Chick holder
24 Stupefy
25 Animal's end part
26 False name
27 Furry
28 Kind of knife
29 Kinds of stars
30 Barbecue
33 Jargon
35 Woo
40 Intoxicated
41 Experience
42 Deviates
43 Cold medicine
45 Business abbr.
47 Paddle
49 Friend
50 Wind
51 Well
52 Economics abrv.
53 Get better
54 Center
55 Impair
56 Otherwise
59 Billion years

**ACROSS**

1 Pass
5 Rock
9 Kimono
13 Drug doer
14 Type of communication
15 Fencing sword
16 Southeast by east
17 Island
18 Bluish green
19 Don't touch (2 wds.)
21 __ curiae
23 Musky
24 Part of the "KKK"
25 Member of an American Indian people
28 Mooring line destination
31 Part of the eye
32 Err
34 Italian currency
36 Be
37 Movie 2001's talking computer
38 Dignitary
39 Parody
41 Moses' mountain
43 Coat
44 Given a new title
46 Arrested
48 U.S. Air Force
49 Satiated
50 Time periods
53 Made hard to find
57 Assignment
58 "__ ho!"
60 Whirl
61 Invalidated
62 Kellogg's waffles
63 Stink
64 Healing plant
65 Sulky
66 Reasonable

**DOWN**

1 Silence
2 At sea
3 Compass point
4 Scoops
5 Green
6 First letter of the Arabic alphabet
7 Animal doc
8 Direction of an axis
9 Relating to the retina
10 Organization of Petroleum Exporting Countries
11 Swain
12 Snaky fish
14 Doubting __ (an apostle)
20 Pouch
22 Bad (prefix)
24 Australian bear
25 Asian nation
26 Mistake
27 Relative
28 Mark
29 Foe
30 Use a car
33 Crook
35 Imitated
40 Fist part
41 Bashed
42 Hardens
43 Sneaks
45 Fire remains
47 Boxer Muhammad
49 Approval
50 Volcano
51 N.T. prophet
52 Capital of Norway
53 Prego's competition
54 Belief
55 Paradise
56 Dam
59 Self

**ACROSS**

1 Baby's bed
5 Prayer ending
9 Wine bottle
13 Angel's head ring
14 Extra tire
15 Cain killed him
16 Plain
17 Assume
18 Small breads
19 Muscat wine
21 Gargantuan
23 Sonata
24 Plateau
25 Displayer of emotions
28 Deplores
31 Lad
32 Doors
34 Shipshape
36 Ozone
37 Vane direction
38 Abridged (abbr.)
39 Luge
41 Giant in 'Princess Bride'
43 Big hairdo
44 Workplaces

46 Hunted animal
48 Potter's oven
49 Entry
50 Arm covering
53 Regions
57 Stave off
58 Movie "King"
60 Adjoin
61 Bullets
62 Sandwich cookies brand
63 Enjoy
64 Sport group
65 Salamander
66 Ooze

**DOWN**

1 Friend
2 Prego's competition
3 Evils
4 Refuse patronage of
5 Niches
6 Mangle
7 Stray
8 Brother's sons
9 Barter
10 Band instrument

11 Narrate
12 Member of an alliance
14 Stitch
20 Copy
22 North American nation
24 Measure
25 Omelette need
26 What you eat
27 Beginning
28 Ties
29 Green
30 Sword
33 Xe
35 Walked
40 Duchy
41 Airfoil on airplane wing
42 Time periods
43 In the air (pl.)
45 Division (abbr.)
47 Spoil
49 Place for storage
50 Spank
51 Maimed
52 Writer Bombeck
53 Killed
54 Off-Broadway award
55 Use a microwave
56 Stair
59 Be

**ACROSS**

1 Hook part
5 Sit
9 Transparent substance
13 Seaweed substance
14 Bake unshelled eggs
15 Computer picture button
16 Taboo
17 Passion
18 Comedian Jay
19 Scrambler of yolks (2 wds.)
21 Saturated
23 Brief letter
24 Southeast by east
25 Sledge
28 Strict persons
31 Dinner drink
32 Several feet
34 Trigger
36 Abridged (abbr.)
37 Distress call
38 Vane direction
39 Not cons
41 African country
43 Tie shoes
44 Spanish fortress commander
46 Lurk
48 Hoopla
49 Eagerness
50 Flitch
53 Grinning
57 Object
58 Deduce
60 Cain killed him
61 Definite
62 Bowed
63 Scoff
64 Acquired Immune Deficiency Syndrome (abbr.)
65 Dam
66 Paradise

**DOWN**

1 Blight
2 Excited
3 Called
4 Pixy
5 Cycle
6 Pit noise
7 __ Lanka
8 Pencil removers
9 Meekest
10 Chilled
11 Pine tree product
12 Soon
14 Forge
20 Porker
22 Kimono sash
24 Soapy
25 Exchange
26 Constellation
27 Enter
28 Examine
29 Foot the bill
30 From that time
33 Side note
35 Look
40 Shams
41 Listening technique (2 wds.)
42 Associated
43 Being connected
45 Sailor's yes
47 Paddle
49 Master of ceremonies
50 Permission to enter a foreign country
51 Decorative needle case
52 Smart person
53 Drink through a straw
54 As previously cited
55 Northeast by east
56 Dale
59 Parch

**ACROSS**

1 University (abbr.)
5 Wading bird
9 Unruly child
13 Rolled chocolate candy brand
14 Sell illegally
15 Every
16 Night light
17 "To __ Mockingbird" (2 wds.)
18 Region
19 Stabled
21 Most uncommon
23 "Mister" (German)
24 Soaring plaything
25 Show off
28 Make nervous
31 Isolated
32 Express indifference
34 Talk back
36 Chick holder
37 Abridged (abbr.)
38 Shoshonean
39 Deception
41 Toothbrush brand
43 Dale
44 Scorn
46 Altered
48 Cowboy apparel
49 Cob
50 Evil spirit
53 Sequined
57 Howl with laughter
58 Christ's disciple
60 Clouded
61 Green Gables dweller
62 Quickly
63 Land measurement
64 Penury
65 "You can't eat just one" brand
66 Alcoholic beverage

**DOWN**

1 Torso extensions
2 Bird
3 Healing plant
4 Phil ___ (Talk show host)
5 Colder
6 Hairless
7 Ailing
8 Saving
9 Couriers
10 Scarce
11 Pros
12 Not this
14 Circumbents
20 Thief's hideout
22 Dined
24 Ridged surface
25 Traveled by airplane
26 Reasoning
27 __ Saxon
28 Not rural
29 Spring
30 Sugar-free brand
33 Wounds
35 Mail
40 Lasted
41 Freud's ___ complex
42 Caution
43 Yarn-dyed cotton cloth
45 Basin
47 Newsman Rather
49 Glasses
50 Persia
51 Not any
52 Sugar plant
53 Wait
54 Tie shoes
55 Jewish scribe
56 Tinted
59 Government agency

**ACROSS**

1 Route
5 Man
9 Shipshape
13 __ Minor (Little Dipper)
14 Type of communication
15 Bored
16 White fruit
17 Island
18 Casing
19 Nocturnal S African dog
21 Sundial pointer
23 Right-winger
24 Lock partners
25 North of downtown
28 Person with knowledge in specific field
31 Ooze
32 Quick
34 Chopped
36 Compass point
37 Time period
38 Past
39 Reserve Officers Training Corps.
41 Type of car
43 Eagerness
44 Rainy
46 Earth's crust
48 Green seedless plant
49 Body appendages
50 Tear out a tree
53 Pistol quieter
57 Destitute
58 Group of eight
60 Dog food brand
61 Upon
62 Starts
63 Feared
64 Loch __ monster
65 Dozes
66 Dregs

**DOWN**

1 Insect in a cocoon
2 Region
3 Tyrant
4 Rigid top on boat
5 Granular
6 First letter of the Arabic alphabet
7 Permit
8 Taxing
9 Cyprus capital
10 Cheese
11 Ditto
12 Adolescent
14 Plant spines
20 Great!
22 New York City
24 Gold weight
25 Soviet Union
26 Spanish coins
27 Chompers
28 Inroad
29 Put on a pedestal
30 Queenly
33 Inheritors
35 Over
40 Country Island group in Indian ocean
41 Leaf garland
42 Melts ore
43 Draw into a tangle
45 Romance
47 Maturity
49 Legal claim
50 Onto
51 Corn bread
52 Decays
53 Stair
54 Hint
55 Fencing sword
56 Poles
59 Accountant

## Crossword Grid

| 1 | 2 | 3 | 4 | ■ | 5 | 6 | 7 | 8 | ■ | 9 | 10 | 11 | 12 |
|---|---|---|---|---|---|---|---|---|---|---|---|---|---|
| 13 | | | | ■ | 14 | | | | ■ | 15 | | | |
| 16 | | | | ■ | 17 | | | | ■ | 18 | | | |
| 19 | | | 20 | | | ■ | 21 | 22 | | | | | |
| ■ | ■ | 23 | | | | ■ | 24 | | | ■ | ■ | ■ | ■ |
| 25 | 26 | 27 | | | ■ | 28 | | | ■ | 29 | 30 | | ■ |
| 31 | | | ■ | 32 | 33 | | | ■ | 34 | | | | 35 |
| 36 | | | ■ | 37 | | | ■ | 38 | | | | | |
| 39 | | | 40 | | 41 | | | 42 | | 43 | | | |
| ■ | 44 | | | 45 | | | ■ | 46 | 47 | | | | |
| ■ | 48 | | | | ■ | 49 | | | | ■ | ■ | ■ | ■ |
| 50 | 51 | 52 | | | ■ | 53 | | | 54 | 55 | 56 | | |
| 57 | | | ■ | 58 | 59 | | | ■ | 60 | | | | |
| 61 | | | ■ | 62 | | | ■ | 63 | | | | | |
| 64 | | | ■ | 65 | | | ■ | 66 | | | | | |

## ACROSS

1 Hook part
5 Sit
9 Transparent substance
13 Seaweed substance
14 Bake unshelled eggs
15 Computer picture button
16 Taboo
17 Passion
18 Comedian Jay
19 Scrambler of yolks (2 wds.)
21 Saturated
23 Brief letter
24 Southeast by east
25 Sledge
28 Strict persons
31 Dinner drink
32 Several feet
34 Trigger
36 Abridged (abbr.)
37 Distress call
38 Vane direction
39 Not cons
41 African country
43 Tie shoes
44 Spanish fortress commander
46 Lurk
48 Hoopla
49 Eagerness
50 Flitch
53 Grinning
57 Object
58 Deduce
60 Cain killed him
61 Definite
62 Bowed
63 Scoff
64 Acquired Immune Deficiency Syndrome (abbr.)
65 Dam
66 Paradise

## DOWN

1 Blight
2 Excited
3 Called
4 Pixy
5 Cycle
6 Pit noise
7 __ Lanka
8 Pencil removers
9 Meekest
10 Chilled
11 Pine tree product
12 Soon
14 Forge
20 Porker
22 Kimono sash
24 Soapy
25 Exchange
26 Constellation
27 Enter
28 Examine
29 Foot the bill
30 From that time
33 Side note
35 Look
40 Shams
41 Listening technique (2 wds.)
42 Associated
43 Being connected
45 Sailor's yes
47 Paddle
49 Master of ceremonies
50 Permission to enter a foreign country
51 Decorative needle case
52 Smart person
53 Drink through a straw
54 As previously cited
55 Northeast by east
56 Dale
59 Parch

**ACROSS**

1 University (abbr.)
5 Wading bird
9 Unruly child
13 Rolled chocolate candy brand
14 Sell illegally
15 Every
16 Night light
17 "To __ Mockingbird" (2 wds.)
18 Region
19 Stabled
21 Most uncommon
23 "Mister" (German)
24 Soaring plaything
25 Show off
28 Make nervous
31 Isolated
32 Express indifference
34 Talk back
36 Chick holder
37 Abridged (abbr.)
38 Shoshonean
39 Deception
41 Toothbrush brand

43 Dale
44 Scorn
46 Altered
48 Cowboy apparel
49 Cob
50 Evil spirit
53 Sequined
57 Howl with laughter
58 Christ's disciple
60 Clouded
61 Green Gables dweller
62 Quickly
63 Land measurement
64 Penury
65 "You can't eat just one" brand
66 Alcoholic beverage

**DOWN**

1 Torso extensions
2 Bird
3 Healing plant
4 Phil ___ (Talk show host)
5 Colder
6 Hairless

7 Ailing
8 Saving
9 Couriers
10 Scarce
11 Pros
12 Not this
14 Circumbents
20 Thief's hideout
22 Dined
24 Ridged surface
25 Traveled by airplane
26 Reasoning
27 __ Saxon
28 Not rural
29 Spring
30 Sugar-free brand
33 Wounds
35 Mail
40 Lasted
41 Freud's ___ complex
42 Caution
43 Yarn-dyed cotton cloth
45 Basin
47 Newsman Rather
49 Glasses
50 Persia
51 Not any
52 Sugar plant
53 Wait
54 Tie shoes
55 Jewish scribe
56 Tinted
59 Government agency

## ACROSS

1 Route
5 Man
9 Shipshape
13 __ Minor (Little Dipper)
14 Type of communication
15 Bored
16 White fruit
17 Island
18 Casing
19 Nocturnal S African dog
21 Sundial pointer
23 Right-winger
24 Lock partners
25 North of downtown
28 Person with knowledge in specific field
31 Ooze
32 Quick
34 Chopped
36 Compass point
37 Time period
38 Past
39 Reserve Officers Training Corps.
41 Type of car
43 Eagerness
44 Rainy
46 Earth's crust
48 Green seedless plant
49 Body appendages
50 Tear out a tree
53 Pistol quieter
57 Destitute
58 Group of eight
60 Dog food brand
61 Upon
62 Starts
63 Feared
64 Loch __ monster
65 Dozes
66 Dregs

## DOWN

1 Insect in a cocoon
2 Region
3 Tyrant
4 Rigid top on boat
5 Granular
6 First letter of the Arabic alphabet
7 Permit
8 Taxing
9 Cyprus capital
10 Cheese
11 Ditto
12 Adolescent
14 Plant spines
20 Great!
22 New York City
24 Gold weight
25 Soviet Union
26 Spanish coins
27 Chompers
28 Inroad
29 Put on a pedestal
30 Queenly
33 Inheritors
35 Over
40 Country Island group in Indian ocean
41 Leaf garland
42 Melts ore
43 Draw into a tangle
45 Romance
47 Maturity
49 Legal claim
50 Onto
51 Corn bread
52 Decays
53 Stair
54 Hint
55 Fencing sword
56 Poles
59 Accountant

**ACROSS**

1 Not many (2 wds.)
5 Giant
9 Garden tools
13 Mere
14 Around
15 European monetary unit
16 Cheese
17 Small Mediterranean boat
18 Land mass
19 Lichen (2 wds.)
21 Horse's head piece
23 Challenge
24 Fuzz
25 Revolve
28 Beanie (2 wds.)
31 Out
32 Catapult
34 365 days
36 Pinch
37 Drag
38 South by east
39 Had known
41 Moses' brother
43 Hour
44 Granny
46 Crustacean
48 Prima donna
49 Dirty area
50 Interfere
53 Peptide like
57 Opaque gem
58 Put a rope through a hole
60 Musical repeat
61 Ecological communities
62 Uncovered
63 Always
64 Incline
65 Take by surprise
66 Deceased

**DOWN**

1 Shorten (abbr.)
2 Gambling game
3 Little Mermaid's love
4 Friday
5 Very fat
6 Lots
7 Regret
8 Engraving
9 Well
10 Depose
11 Canal
12 Surge
14 Atlantic islands
20 Entrance rug
22 Whichever
24 Jargon
25 Stink
26 Due
27 Point
28 Jeweled headdress
29 Fable writer
30 No-no
33 South American animal
35 Rive
40 Walked like a duck
41 Modifiers
42 Took a small bite
43 Discovered
45 Nada
47 Drunk
49 A small number
50 Greatest amount
51 Fencing sword
52 Exclamation
53 South American country
54 Noah's bird
55 Belief
56 Roster
59 Feed

**ACROSS**

1 Lay in the sun
5 Second letter of the greek alphabet
9 Space administration
13 Economics abrv.
14 Light purple flower
15 Wading bird
16 Citizen
17 Open mouthed
18 Snaky fish
19 Seven sides
21 Tattle (2 wds.)
23 Clip
24 Lubricates
25 Must (2 wds.)
28 Endures
31 Eager
32 ___ gritty
34 Dozes
36 Pole
37 Big truck
38 Twosome
39 Vessel
41 Giver
43 Energy
44 Making dirty
46 Musician
48 Sympathize with
49 Adjoin
50 Mary's husband
53 Ornamental wall ridging
57 Onto
58 Mistake
60 Scent
61 Quarry
62 Cook with dry heat
63 Change residences
64 Luge
65 Southeast by east
66 Murder

**DOWN**

1 Elizabeth's nickname
2 Hurt
3 Day time tv show
4 Purled
5 Prejudiced person
6 Eagerness
7 Pierce
8 To change into vinegar
9 TV rating
10 Cain killed him
11 Grainery
12 Association (abbr.)
14 Shallow pond
20 Artist's creation
22 Fairy
24 Expenditure
25 Rabbit
26 Expresses
27 Movie on tape
28 Hurt
29 Radiuses
30 Cowboy boot projections
33 Humor
35 Arrange
40 Matured
41 Frets
42 Mr. Redford
43 Glen
45 Kisser's need
47 Large vehicle
49 Woken
50 Containers
51 Opaque gem
52 Few
53 Little Mermaid's Sebastian
54 Teen hero
55 Star
56 Color
59 Caviar

**ACROSS**

1 Wash
5 Broth
9 Financial obligation
13 Decoy
14 Pace
15 Fencing sword
16 Spoken
17 Grab
18 National capital
19 Run for office
21 Of the laity
23 Giant
24 Small town
25 Put more gas in
28 Excavating vehicle
31 Except
32 Tiny particle
34 Cab
36 Condemn
37 Past
38 Melancholy
39 Volcano
41 Weighted fishnet
43 Small mountain
44 Baseball bat company

46 Frothy
48 Lowest in rank
49 Jessica's nickname
50 Impart
53 Common side order
57 Little Mermaid's love
58 Headquarters of British India
60 Fancy car
61 Stroke
62 Improve
63 Tied
64 Perceives with eye
65 Carpets
66 Nick

**DOWN**

1 Alliance
2 Manner
3 Trolley car
4 Assist (2 wds.)
5 Sew together
6 Bode
7 United Parcel Service
8 Shared dinner
9 Please

10 Great
11 Torah table
12 Bluish green
14 Spins around
20 Maturity
22 ___ of the covenant
24 Pork
25 Kimono
26 Show emotions
27 Female singer ____ Apple
28 Initiate
29 Desert pond
30 Put on a pedestal
33 Song of praise
35 Lazily
40 Features
41 Burn with little smoke
42 Facial part
43 Bothered
45 Oolong
47 Vane direction
49 Port-a-potties
50 Cincinnati baseball team
51 Canal
52 Wandering plant
53 Fly
54 Reside
55 Prayer ending
56 Accustomed
59 Flightless bird

## ACROSS

1 Wash
5 Asian dress
9 Stagger
13 Land mass
14 Express indifference
15 Au naturel
16 Oracle
17 Men's counterparts
   Ladies
18 Part of the eye
19 From screen to paper
21 Blocks of metal
23 Duces
24 Western state
25 Rich person
28 Unskillfully
31 Glean
32 First course
34 Chimney dirt
36 Paddle
37 Evergreen tree
38 Purchase
39 Colorless
41 Corset
43 Angel's instrument
44 Pounded feet
46 Gruff
48 Cold person's noise
49 Stabs
50 Blood part
53 Legal
57 Pacify
58 I __ if I could
60 Italian currency
61 Band instrument
62 Alleys
63 Extremely long time
   periods
64 Accomplishment
65 Finish
66 Nick

## DOWN

1 Big party
2 At sea
3 Degree
4 Rigid top on boat
5 Small stores
6 Navy's rival
7 Regret
8 Caught fire
9 Men in shining armor
10 European monetary unit
11 Blue-pencil
12 Not as much
14 Faints
20 Cash with order (abr.)
22 Snooze
24 Single
25 Walked
26 Many months
27 Weight unit
28 Book by Homer
29 Rounded part
30 Belonging to you
33 Behind
35 Use a keyboard
40 Fast toboggan
41 Spreads out
42 Splinters of glass
43 Bothered
45 Untalkative
47 Kimono sash
49 Mixed drink
50 Walk slowly
51 Lubricate
52 Healing plant
53 Hera
54 Wear out
55 Persia
56 Molded
59 Cereal

**ACROSS**

1 Karma
5 Among
9 Sailors "hey"
13 Persia
14 Swamp
15 Star
16 River dirt
17 Void
18 Ajar
19 Spanish estate
21 Consignment
23 Scratch
24 Fatty
25 Serious
28 Sunshades
31 Two good friends
32 Fearing
34 Food
36 Also known as (abbr.)
37 Poem
38 Cc
39 Note
41 Each
43 Capital of Vanuatu
44 Locals

46 Publicly
48 Matching
49 Goofs
50 Educate
53 Upsets (2 wds.)
57 Threaten
58 Remove
60 Relive
61 __ Minor (Little Dipper)
62 Speaker
63 Legal claim to property
64 Paradise
65 Duces
66 Strip

**DOWN**

1 Trawl
2 Opera solo
3 Baby powder
4 Tempts
5 Root beer brand (3 wds.)
6 Starling
7 Note of debt
8 Blunting
9 Relieving pain
10 N.A. Indian

11 Baker's need
12 Yin's partner
14 Yellow fruit
20 Tree
22 Boxer Muhammad
24 Possessor
25 Canned meat brand
26 Similar to oak
27 South American animal
28 Assistants
29 Urchin
30 Not moving
33 Like cloth
35 Murder
40 Turkish
41 Worst
42 New __ (Big Apple dweller)
43 Buckets
45 The other half of Jima
47 Before (prefix)
49 Comforts
50 Veer
51 Lacing
52 Flexible tube
53 Condiment
54 Send by post
55 At sea
56 Nick
59 Underdone

## ACROSS

1 Revere
5 U.S. Department of Agriculture
9 Tense
13 Track
14 Dido
15 Fly alone
16 Deeds
17 Composer Francis __ Key
18 Trigonometry
19 Wave crest
21 Parallelograms
23 Stair
24 Blood carrier
25 Buckeye State resident
28 Famous chapel
31 AM
32 Demonstrations
34 Nearly horizontal entrance
36 Government agency
37 Volume (abbr.)
38 Self
39 Meshes
41 Summary
43 Pros
44 Reconsider
46 Proposes
48 Mob activity
49 Hint
50 Had a dream
53 From Ghana
57 Gem
58 Vegetable
60 Kimono
61 Healing plant
62 Uninvited
63 Vessel
64 Fold
65 Oracle
66 Pedestal part

## DOWN

1 Defect
2 Every
3 Negative (prefix)
4 Leans (2 wds.)
5 Take off the lid
6 Finish
7 Telegraphic signal
8 Female Performer
9 Baltic country
10 Residence hall
11 Voluble
12 Bear or Berra
14 Go up
20 Estimated time of arrival
22 Whack
24 Bowed stringed instrument
25 Bode
26 Wisher
27 Wrathful
28 Duster
29 Relative
30 Lawn tool
33 Natural occurrence
35 Throw in the air
40 Roamed
41 Rebellious
42 European country
43 Afraid
45 That man
47 Frolic
49 Singing group
50 Colorless
51 Judge
52 Black
53 Scoff
54 Midwestern state
55 Bedroom furniture (2 wds.)
56 Roman emperor
59 Compass point

**ACROSS**

1 Bullet
5 African country
9 __ and span
13 Space administration
14 Creator of Sherlock Holmes
15 Engage
16 Affirm
17 Number system base
18 Economics abrv.
19 Stone, Gutter creatures
21 Czar
23 Country in SE Asia
24 Baby's bed
25 Capital of Lesotho
28 Buxom
31 Swiss mountains
32 After bath need
34 Has toed
36 Central Intelligence Agency
37 Game official
38 Compass point
39 Impair
41 __ alarm
43 Fast airplanes
44 Shoreline embankment
46 Jacket
48 Small fresh water fish
49 Decorative needle case
50 Baseball's Strawberry
53 Fairness
57 Region
58 Tropical American mammal
60 Clip
61 Asian nation
62 Doors
63 National capital
64 Rabbit
65 Factor of ten
66 365 days

**DOWN**

1 Hang-up
2 Rock
3 Drug doer
4 Used mouthwash
5 Hot embers
6 Dr. Jekyll's "partner"
7 Boxer Muhammad
8 Dexter
9 Fruit ice cream
10 Typesetting measurement
11 Take the wrinkles out
12 Penny
14 Parch (2 wds.)
20 Paddle
22 Shrill bark
24 Cooks
25 Speed
26 False name
27 Extra tire
28 Peachy
29 Individualist
30 Gossiper
33 Toothbrush brand
35 Office furniture
40 Patterned knot tying knot
41 Marred
42 Diners
43 United manner
45 Reporter's question
47 Abbess
49 1997 Madonna movie
50 Dart
51 Opera solo
52 Tush
53 Great
54 Canal
55 Bod
56 Heavenly light
59 Wood chopper

**ACROSS**

1 6th month (Jewish calendar)
5 Water (Sp.)
9 Priggish
13 Note
14 Hurt
15 Past times
16 Tub spread
17 National capital
18 Adventure story
19 Relatives
21 A, for example
23 Real
24 What a clock tells
25 Descend by repelling
28 Asphalt origin
31 Look
32 Fancy round mat
34 Veer
36 Stray
37 Bundle
38 Cook
39 Doe
41 Bay
43 Ascend
44 Tram
46 Did penitence
48 Meek
49 Skins
50 Asian fiber plant
53 Bonsai (2 wds.)
57 Decorative needle case
58 Rejoice
60 Part of a ladder
61 Soon
62 Fathers
63 Reverse
64 Called
65 Sieve
66 Dining hall

**DOWN**

1 Berserk
2 Cafe
3 Prayer ending
4 Cock
5 Dickens' "__ of Two Cities" (2 wds.)
6 Sticky goop
7 Spanish "one"
8 Quickness
9 Methods
10 Castle canal
11 Advise
12 Cogged wheel
14 Ought
20 Friday (abbr.)
22 Flightless bird
24 Typographic character
25 Imitated
26 Small hat
27 Dried up
28 Onion roll
29 Mischievous
30 Hospital worker
33 Held the deed
35 Looked
40 Playing noisily
41 Malady
42 Mocks
43 Beaklike or snoutlike projection
45 Tell a tall tale
47 Sample
49 Lace of square mesh
50 What you do to a sound
51 Volcano
52 Electron, for example
53 Sward
54 Ancien German character
55 Ceases
56 Self-esteems
59 Roman dozen

The grid (crossword puzzle grid with numbered cells).

## ACROSS

1 Joyful
5 Plateau
9 Scent
13 Greek god of war
14 Light purple flower
15 Brand of milk
16 Ooze
17 Expression
18 Tied
19 Capital is Islamabad
21 Czar
23 Decays
24 Carol
25 Submissive
28 Sense perceived
31 Onto
32 Synthetic fabric
34 Not whites
36 Central Intelligence Agency
37 Cask
38 Decade
39 Ballet skirt
41 Headquarters of British India
43 Smile location
44 Muezzin locale
46 Sleek
48 Weight unit
49 Opera solo
50 Popular Japanese drama
53 Truck driver
57 Island
58 Lasso
60 Tropical edible root
61 Legal claim to property
62 Enter
63 Doorway sign
64 Firm
65 Insightful
66 Game cubes

## DOWN

1 Puff
2 Region
3 Onion-like vegetable
4 Early pain relieving drug
5 Muffler company
6 Eagerness
7 Droop
8 Solvent for making rayon
9 Veneer
10 Prima donna
11 Baker's need
12 Jabber
14 Last
20 Sun's name
22 Affirmation
24 Horse sound
25 Canal
26 Narcotic
27 Raccoon-like animal
28 Melt ore
29 Add
30 Chosen
33 BB Player Abdul Jabar
35 Leg joint
40 Balm
41 Exhausted
42 Asian nation
43 Stuffed self with food
45 __ of the covenant
47 Good health
49 Fable writer
50 Scottish skirt
51 Land mass
52 Type of cheese
53 Ripped up
54 Cab
55 Little Mermaid's love
56 Memorization
59 Only

## Crossword Grid

| 1 | 2 | 3 | 4 | | | 5 | 6 | 7 | 8 | | 9 | 10 | 11 | 12 |
|---|---|---|---|---|---|---|---|---|---|---|---|---|---|---|

*(grid with numbered cells)*

**ACROSS**

1 Wind
5 Decorative needle case
9 Give
13 Angel's head ring
14 Treat
15 Spool
16 Gets older
17 Ice house
18 Charity
19 Lip hair
21 Child
23 Baseball glove
24 Caps
25 Sports car brand
28 Chugs
31 Against
32 Chop up
34 Sweet potatoes
36 Internal Revenue Service
37 Cab
38 Twitching
39 Penury
41 Uttered
43 Soft cheese from Greece
44 Hamper
46 Wage getter
48 What a bald man is missing
49 Churned water from a boat
50 Color intensity
53 Flails
57 Dining or living ending
58 Cook meat
60 Angel's instrument
61 Band instrument
62 Truck
63 Jewish scribe
64 Pokey
65 Vessel
66 Bird's home

**DOWN**

1 Whop
2 Prego's competition
3 Brews
4 Mailman
5 Number
6 Myth
7 Spanish "one"
8 Revere
9 Offensively
10 Snaky fish
11 Prefix for half
12 Otherwise
14 One that was hurt
20 Atmosphere
22 Cutting tool
24 Money
25 Disposed
26 Heron
27 Bleacher
28 Tree knot
29 Dine
30 Strike hard
33 Colder
35 Pock
40 Former name for Benin
41 Good-natured
42 "You'll pay __ for this!"
43 ___ up before dinner, get cleaned up
45 Mayan
47 Also known as (abbr.)
49 Purr
50 Harvest
51 Homeless person
52 Castle
53 Ripped up
54 Fog
55 Goofs
56 Lovers quarrel
59 Affray

Crossword grid with numbered cells (1–66).

**ACROSS**

1 Invitation abbreviaton
5 Turfs
9 Defect
13 Buckeye State
14 Tan color
15 That hurts!
16 Knife
17 "__ Dame"
18 Gumbo
19 Small birds
21 Cash in
23 Babe
24 Forehead
25 Inter
28 Pencil removers
31 Not one
32 Up or down on a graph
34 Hairless
36 Stamping tool
37 Cut of beef
38 Collection of animals
39 Strip
41 Restrain
43 Idiot
44 Stresses
46 Listener
48 __ Minor (Little Dipper)
49 Gal
50 NE French region
53 Someone who sits on a panel
57 Legal claim to property
58 Philippine dish with marinated chicken or pork
60 Not out of
61 Organization of Petroleum Exporting Countries
62 Hawks
63 Economics abrv.
64 Spot
65 Women's magazine
66 Knocks (2 wds.)

**DOWN**

1 Loots
2 Buy
3 Capital of Vanuatu
4 Hoagie (2 wds.)
5 Fancy
6 Grain
7 Danish krone (abbr.)
8 Mountains
9 Ecological food chain (2 wds.)
10 N.T. book
11 Land measurement
12 Whop
14 Nodal
20 Cram
22 Aurora
24 Pay to keep quiet
25 Ceases
26 What a hammer hits
27 Foot the bill
28 Doors
29 Shaving tool
30 Tilt
33 Athletic field
35 Worker
40 Absent without permission
41 Gout
42 Large african animals, for short
43 Lager
45 Spark
47 Bard's before
49 Dormer
50 Healing plant
51 Mouth parts
52 Ooze
53 Count votes
54 S.A. Indian
55 Finish
56 Loads
59 Delaware

Atlantic Ocean
10 6th month (Jewish calendar)
11 Run easily
12 Wilma Flintstones' husband
14 Philosophical people
20 Luau dish
22 Paddle
24 Throat infection
25 Plateau
26 Alpha's opposite
27 Building place
28 More tender
29 Spooky
30 Scare
33 Enlarge
35 Do it again
40 Residential districts
41 Near the kidneys
42 Spiny
43 Led
45 Neither's partner
47 Extremely high frequency (abbr.)
49 Hearkens
50 Association (abbr.)
51 Isolated
52 Country in SE Asia
53 Small ground plot
54 Tropical island
55 Women's magazine
56 Oceans
59 Roberto's yes

**ACROSS**

1 Tennis player Steffi
5 A wager (2 wds.)
9 Leg muscle
13 Space administration
14 Quoth
15 Scent
16 Drug doer
17 Movie character Dick
18 Back of the neck
19 Hair soaps
21 Made a menacing noise
23 Nickel
24 Saturate
25 Tile art
28 Moved
31 Shine
32 Hand weapon
34 365 days
36 Adjust
37 Wrath
38 Regret
39 Gets older
41 Skillful
43 Oblige
44 Into parts

46 To this document
48 Came into life
49 Santa call (2 wds.)
50 Attract
53 Woman's colognes
57 Surge
58 Mr. Ryan
60 Wind
61 Stuck up person
62 Wing shaped
63 __ hoop (child's toy)
64 Loch __ monster
65 Allows
66 Binds

**DOWN**

1 African antelope
2 Madcap
3 At sea
4 Barnyard mouser (2 wds.)
5 Moses' brother
6 Prejudice
7 And so forth
8 Neck gland
9 Capital of Guinea on

**ACROSS**

- **1** Male deer
- **5** Pit noise
- **9** Pops
- **13** Real
- **14** Bobbin
- **15** Tied
- **16** Am not
- **17** Metric linear unit
- **18** Unconsciousness
- **19** African nation
- **21** Insect
- **23** Western Athletic Conferences
- **24** Want
- **25** Adorn
- **28** Dozer
- **31** Doorway sign
- **32** American indian
- **34** Animal's end part
- **36** Extension (abbr.)
- **37** Hoary
- **38** Also
- **39** Dorothy's dog
- **41** Pig pens
- **43** Allows
- **44** Tablet
- **46** Unwilling
- **48** Sticky black substances
- **49** Animal insect
- **50** No longer asea
- **53** Foot step sound
- **57** Injure
- **58** Nut
- **60** Opera solo
- **61** Gumbo
- **62** Chimes
- **63** Musky
- **64** Was looked at
- **65** Satiate
- **66** Tides

**DOWN**

- **1** Poke
- **2** Three
- **3** Father's sister
- **4** Soaks (2 wds.)
- **5** Starts
- **6** Small particle
- **7** Neither's partner
- **8** Nose tissue
- **9** Decode
- **10** Assure
- **11** Prefix for half
- **12** Hang-up
- **14** Kisses
- **20** Western Athletic Conference
- **22** Avenue
- **24** Escape
- **25** Root vegetable
- **26** Gas company
- **27** Also
- **28** Fixed
- **29** Food consumer
- **30** What a mob does
- **33** Tiny amounts
- **35** Mislay
- **40** Turkish
- **41** Unfolds
- **42** Hair cutting place
- **43** Foliage
- **45** Hearing part
- **47** Animal doc
- **49** __ ahead
- **50** Famous cookies
- **51** Interest
- **52** Engage
- **53** Baptismal __
- **54** Middle East dweller
- **55** Tree branch
- **56** "You can't eat just one" brand
- **59** Central Intelligence Agency

**ACROSS**

1 Father
5 Tennis player Steffi
9 Drains energy
13 Animal oil
14 Will
15 Spoken
16 Proper
17 Organized crime
18 African river
19 Submissive
21 McDonald's clown
23 Costa __
24 Waiting place
25 Expose
28 Hereditary
31 Taint
32 Canned chili brand
34 Priggish
36 Those who make the food laws (abbr.)
37 Back to school mo.
38 Women's undergarment
39 Dalai __
41 Anxiety
43 Canal name
44 Driver's permit
46 Occlude
48 Italian boy's name
49 Beef
50 Adjust
53 Hare beater
57 Italian currency
58 Adapted to a dry environment
60 Tyrant
61 Small ground plot
62 Eat away
63 Chowder ingredient
64 Eye infection
65 Removes the water
66 Juno

**DOWN**

1 Dog food brand
2 Hook part
3 Cheese
4 Navy Rank
5 African nation
6 Log boat
7 Boxer Muhammad
8 Blazing
9 14 line poems
10 Opera solo
11 Satiate
12 Luge
14 Kisses
20 Bro.'s sibling
22 Only
24 No Nonsense competitor
25 Defunct football league
26 Knobby
27 __ Vice (tv show)
28 Measuring device
29 Soak
30 Recovered
33 Bitter herb
35 Stare
40 Start
41 Added on
42 Third part
43 Blotch
45 Billion years
47 Entrance rug
49 Nothingness
50 Swiss mountains
51 Slope
52 What waiters carry
53 Helen of __
54 Island
55 France & Germany river
56 Writer Bombeck
59 Stray

**ACROSS**

1 Baths
5 Mix
9 Onto
13 Dirt dweller
14 Swamp
15 Northeast by east
16 At sea
17 Data
18 What a bald man is missing
19 Self-righteous hypocrite
21 Followed
23 Degree
24 Gait
25 Phasic
28 Faultfinding
31 Slimly
32 Pluck
34 Angel's head ring
36 Unpaid
37 Business abbr.
38 Strike sharply
39 Bend
41 Hawaiian 'hello'
43 Unconsciousness
44 Hone
46 Relating to spring
48 Cheats
49 Gambling game
50 Club
53 Unselfish concern
57 Spoken
58 Sleep disorder
60 Dorothy's dog
61 Leer at
62 Whoop
63 Unpaid
64 Penury
65 Pulpit
66 Label

**DOWN**

1 Exchange
2 Fashionable
3 Region
4 Wisely
5 Not as nuts
6 Use a keyboard
7 Note of debt
8 Furrowing
9 Take trailer off truck
10 Clang
11 Off-Broadway award
12 Smart person
14 Cut in half
20 Three
22 Boxer Muhammad
24 Type of mob
25 Musical repeat
26 Belonging to you
27 Slavonic language
28 Cathedral's clergyman
29 Moses' brother
30 South American animal
33 Cunnings
35 Opaque gem
40 Dickered
41 Clap
42 Ideal person
43 Salad topping
45 Grain
47 Stray
49 Takes off
50 Racoon's nickname
51 Advise
52 Glen
53 Negative (prefix)
54 Midwestern state
55 Prow
56 Particular form
59 School group

The grid (numbered crossword puzzle cells):

Row 1: 1, 2, 3, 4, ■, 5, 6, 7, 8, ■, 9, 10, 11, 12
Row 2: 13, 14, ■, 15
Row 3: 16, 17, ■, 18
Row 4: 19, 20, 21, 22
Row 5: 23, 24
Row 6: 25, 26, 27, 28, 29, 30
Row 7: 31, 32, 33, 34, 35
Row 8: 36, 37, 38
Row 9: 39, 40, 41, 42, 43
Row 10: 44, 45, 46, 47
Row 11: 48, 49
Row 12: 50, 51, 52, 53, 54, 55, 56
Row 13: 57, 58, 59, 60
Row 14: 61, 62, 63
Row 15: 64, 65, 66

## ACROSS

1 Wait
5 Homeless person
9 Bode
13 Roman cloaks
14 Demobilize
15 Natural enclosure
16 Western state
17 Silly
18 Aegis
19 New England Dialect
21 Slow, shelled animals
23 Pasta
24 MGM's leo
25 Assent
28 Russian Kathy
31 Untied
32 Swell
34 Point
36 Crimson
37 Pain unit
38 Cell stuff
39 Opaque gem
41 Fathers
43 Jetty
44 Builder
46 Relating to a choir
48 Pod vegetables
49 Fuel
50 Railways
53 Relating to Greece
57 Dunking cookies
58 Amass
60 Science
61 In __ of
62 Pixies
63 Belief
64 Optical device
65 Perceives with eye
66 Bivouac

## DOWN

1 Take by surprise
2 Dorothy's dog
3 Seaweed substance
4 Dice game
5 ___ Matisse, painter
6 Asian country
7 __ fire
8 Fatness
9 Vast
10 Wise Man
11 Cruel
12 Loch __ monster
14 Tried to lose weight
20 Concealed
22 Neither's partner
24 Scoop out
25 Big hairdo
26 Thin pancake
27 Wood
28 Seasoner makers
29 Lowest point
30 Sleep disorder
33 Bye
35 Royalty
40 Having leprosy
41 Hoards
42 Chews out
43 Debate
45 Executive
47 Movie 2001's talking computer
49 Demeter
50 Gangster's girlfriend
51 Canal
52 Adolescent
53 Own
54 Naught
55 Object
56 Fellow
59 Roberto's yes

**ACROSS**

1 Weakling
5 Small particle
9 Second letter of the greek alphabet
13 Teen hero
14 Stubble
15 Persia
16 Ecological communities
17 Country house
18 Scottish skirt
19 As much as hands can hold
21 Eave hanger in winter
23 Farside's Larson
24 Soon
25 Falling star
28 Continuing ( 2 wds.)
31 Mined metals
32 Several feet
34 Definite
36 Miner's goal
37 Standard or average
38 Spoil
39 Lug
41 Part of the UK

43 Association (abbr.)
44 Leaf used for pies
46 Mother __
48 Attack
49 Flurry
50 Asian pheasant
53 Toughened
57 Convex shape
58 Assume
60 Pleasant
61 Bearing
62 What is agreed upon
63 Computer picture button
64 Chichi
65 Rice wine
66 Tilt

**DOWN**

1 Expect
2 Belief
3 AM
4 Vows
5 Pope's country
6 Globes
7 Thai
8 Sunshades

9 Two pieces
10 Little Mermaid's love
11 Lanky
12 Wager
14 Scamper
20 Food and Agriculture Organization (abbr.)
22 Murmur
24 Giant in 'Princess Bride'
25 Debate
26 Mistake
27 Chompers
28 Toothbrush brand
29 Hospital worker
30 Yucky
33 Separate
35 Volcano
40 Pleasant combination of sounds
41 Hard shelled nuts
42 Mixes up
43 _____ and Old Lace
45 Stinger
47 Sixth sense
49 Italian physicist
50 Cougar
51 Native ruler
52 A wager (2 wds.)
53 Turkish citizen
54 Costa __
55 Economics abrv.
56 Nick
59 Ocean

**ACROSS**

1 Trawl
5 What children learn
9 Former
13 Small particle
14 Hardhearted
15 Air (prefix)
16 Cob
17 Tie
18 Of no value
19 Spade (2 wds.)
21 Third part
23 Bivouac
24 Net strung across a stream
25 Make camp
28 Food shortages
31 Look
32 Sprinkles white stuff on
34 River dirt
36 Hotel
37 Downwind
38 Directory (abbr.)
39 Compass point
41 Warfs
43 Do it again
44 Injuries
46 Eyed
48 Advise
49 Mind
50 Complainer
53 Simulating
57 Father
58 Great ape
60 Canal
61 Seethe
62 Wise Man's gift
63 Connecticut (abbr.)
64 Monetary unit
65 Partial
66 Leg joint

**DOWN**

1 State treasury
2 Midwestern state
3 Heavenly light
4 Small hand powered railroad car
5 A vacation (2 wds.)
6 Spree
7 Nervous system
8 Methods
9 Bars
10 What you do to a sound
11 Little Mermaid's love
12 Not any
14 Mixes up
20 Surface to air missile
22 Three
24 Dew
25 Otherwise
26 Asian country
27 Come to an end
28 Takes off
29 Bedspread feather
30 Skid
33 Tight at the top, flaring at the bottom (2 wds.)
35 Walked
40 Giant wave
41 Organized massacres
42 Sledge
43 Hick
45 Wrath
47 Electroencephalograph (abbr.)
49 ___ Matisse, painter
50 Welcome rugs
51 Follow
52 Cain killed him
53 Raise crops
54 Take the wrinkles out
55 After eight
56 Heredity component
59 Grain

**ACROSS**

1 Hurt one's toe
5 Pear type
9 Cram
13 Taboo
14 Japanese poem
15 Opaque gem
16 Motor vehicle
17 Improvise a speech
18 Bride's headdress
19 Extends
21 Eave hanger in winter
23 Otherwise
24 Computer picture button
25 Emperor of Japan
28 Malady
31 Paradise
32 Film
34 Ego
36 Beat
37 By way of
38 Hair stuff
39 Soybean
41 Full of swamp grass
43 Traveled by horse
44 Orators
46 City
48 Smooch
49 Tinted
50 Askance
53 Fastening to something
57 Cereal
58 4-H (spelled out)
60 Scent
61 African nation
62 Advises
63 Lug
64 Mined metals
65 Dregs
66 Killed

**DOWN**

1 Fasten
2 What tourists take
3 To
4 Algebra type
5 Symbol
6 Lubricates
7 Slide on snow
8 Stall
9 Cattle
10 Organization of Petroleum Exporting Countries
11 Nab
12 Women's magazine
14 Carriage
20 Hoary
22 Learn from books
24 Book by Homer
25 Cat cries
26 Dummy
27 African country
28 Crawling vines
29 Sego lilies' bulbs
30 Childrens sliding toys
33 Pull__ (sweaters)
35 Animal insect
40 Strong chemical bases
41 Peaceful
42 Juveniles
43 Spicy candy
45 Family
47 December
49 Employs
50 Bullets
51 Scorch
52 Vegetable
53 Giant
54 Teen hero
55 Brief letter
56 Planted
59 Miner's goal

**ACROSS**

1 Hurt one's toe
5 Asian dress
9 Swine
13 Royalty
14 Play a guitar
15 Healing plant
16 Ditto
17 Get ready
18 Lanky
19 Timed
21 Enwrap
23 Nip
24 Traced
25 Tear out a tree
28 The UK
31 Close the door hard
32 Enter
34 Not mine
36 Pop
37 Elver
38 Sample
39 Land mass
41 Squashed circles
43 Space administration
44 Wednesday

46 Got up
48 "Mister" (German)
49 Unruly child
50 Metal fasteners
53 Curriculums
57 Scent
58 Educate
60 Spoken
61 Pamper
62 Looking at
63 Ca. University
64 Luge
65 Say its not true
66 Liner

**DOWN**

1 Clothing stitch
2 Myth
3 __ Minor (Little Dipper)
4 Bloom
5 Throat infection
6 Dry
7 Strong drink
8 Menace
9 Midway
10 Tub spread

11 Destination
12 Mail
14 Fairy
20 Spanish "one"
22 Yield
24 Humorous
25 U.S. Department of Agriculture
26 Plasma
27 Radiuses
28 Hiatus
29 Tiny amounts
30 Hospital worker
33 At no time
35 Baseball's Nolan
40 Stuck
41 Electromagnetism discoverer
42 Skirt
43 ___ oxide (anesthetic)
45 Dewy
47 Newspaper
49 Saline
50 Poles
51 Teen hero
52 Choose
53 Hurt
54 Bend
55 African nation
56 Strike
59 Grain

**ACROSS**

1 Every
5 Syllables used in songs (2 wds.)
9 Baseball team
13 Judge
14 Chest
15 Fencing sword
16 Take the wrinkles out
17 Adjust
18 Pleasant
19 Sing a song a _____ (without instruments)
21 Time periods
23 Straightforward
24 Tyrant
25 Holy places
28 SA alligators
31 Star ___ (tv show)
32 Mediterranean island
34 What a bald man is missing
36 Time period
37 Make lace
38 Wrath
39 Cooking vessels
41 Frozen pizza brand
43 Tied
44 Ahab's profession
46 Silvery
48 Fence opening
49 Fly
50 Genus Alauda
53 Pancake cookers
57 Adventure story
58 Mr. Ryan
60 Midwestern state
61 Heavenly light
62 Silly
63 Gush out
64 Roman emperor
65 Give
66 Possessive pronoun

**DOWN**

1 Little Mermaid's love
2 Manner
3 Clunk
4 Nagging husband (verb)
5 Stupidity
6 Land mass
7 Record
8 Memory loss
9 Jewish candle
10 Great
11 Technical
12 Perceives with eye
14 Ointment
20 Feed
22 Brand of non-stick spray
24 Lousy
25 Stair
26 Cupid's dart
27 Under, poetically
28 Clank
29 Trusting
30 Warning whistle
33 Do penitence
35 Engage
40 Red cactus fruit
41 "Unsinkable ship"
42 Salty
43 Omelet (2 wds.)
45 Child
47 Crimson
49 Heavy machinery
50 Association (abbr.)
51 Tardy
52 Seaweed substance
53 Elated
54 Run easily
55 Vessel
56 Wood cutting tools
59 Only

**ACROSS**

1 Dog food brand
5 Choice
9 Require
13 Told a tall tale
14 Timid boy
15 Hurt
16 Big hairdo
17 Point
18 Hint
19 Solidly
21 Fall
23 Fatty
24 Upon
25 Type of angle
28 Floor cleaner
31 __ ex machina
32 What a snake skin is
34 Little Mermaid's love
36 Often poetically
37 Downwind
38 African antelope
39 Dining or living ending
41 Dreads
43 Part of a football player's gear
44 Ode to this urn
46 What a ghost does
48 Cabana
49 Written material
50 Watch for intruders
53 Duchies
57 Decorative needle case
58 Mud brick
60 Band instrument
61 Reserve Officers Training Corps.
62 Having to do with the navy
63 Telegram
64 Sonata
65 Colors
66 Penury

**DOWN**

1 Alack's partner
2 Heft
3 South American country
4 Smelly
5 Onion roll
6 Spot
7 Compass point
8 Dictator government
9 Milk ingredient
10 Organization concerned with civil liberties (abbr.)
11 Friend
12 Enthusiastic
14 Steps for crossing a fence
20 Hades
22 Shoshonean
24 Cargo vessel
25 Scent
26 Confuse
27 Private instructor
28 Song of praise
29 Musical instrument
30 Gourmet chocolate brand
33 Shoe projection
35 Swear
40 Art of meter writing
41 Country NE Baltic sea
42 Monetary unit
43 Place (2 wds.)
45 Executive
47 Wood chopper
49 Large brass instruments
50 Brand of coffee alternative
51 A spinning toy (2 wds.)
52 Ballet skirt
53 Noah's bird
54 Off-Broadway award
55 Extra
56 Origination
59 24 hours

**ACROSS**

1 Hook part
5 Reverberate
9 Exchange
13 Region
14 Boyfriends
15 Cab
16 Prevaricator
17 Terse
18 Tied
19 Ewe epidermis
21 Giant's wife
23 Canal
24 Elm
25 Famous Russian Ruler
28 Grotesque
31 Draw
32 Sheep-like animals
34 Murder
36 Hoary
37 Cc
38 Prompt
39 Net strung across a stream
41 Cornstalk
43 Second letter of the greek alphabet
44 Potato trait
46 Clothing donner
48 Space administration
49 Toot
50 Renter
53 Sign
57 Store
58 Coral reef
60 Chilled
61 Manner
62 Hawks
63 Shrill noise
64 Covered with ice
65 Harvard's rival
66 Whirl

**DOWN**

1 Sphere
2 Opera solo
3 Stack of paper
4 Muscle builder
5 Spooky
6 Adam's son
7 Shade
8 Shoes
9 Music players
10 Fan
11 Cutting tools
12 Bowler's target
14 Musician (3 wds.)
20 __ Lanka
22 "To the right!"
24 Legend
25 Rerun
26 Fish stories
27 Tax payer's fear
28 Furry
29 Stomache sore
30 Cook with fat
33 City
35 365 days
40 Fled (2 wds.)
41 Joy
42 Inhabits
43 To immerse with water
45 Fled
47 Elver
49 Disney character
50 Tyrant
51 Decorative needle case
52 "Cheers" regular
53 Fee
54 Bad rain
55 Loan
56 Tense
59 Oolong

**ACROSS**

1 Tyrant
5 Wise Man
9 Frozen rain
13 Gumbo
14 Less
15 Meditation
16 Territory held in fee
17 Water retention
18 Blend
19 No fear
21 City
23 Italian currency
24 Nearly horizontal entrance
25 Systematic plan
28 Hollers
31 Praise
32 Deplete
34 Momma
36 Building addition
37 Miner's goal
38 Delaware
39 Droop
41 Cut of beef
43 Hello!
44 Ecological food chain (2 wds.)
46 Re-employ
48 Courts
49 __ Minor (Little Dipper)
50 What a mosquito bite does
53 Different forms of elements
57 Biblical "you"
58 Sort
60 Narrate
61 Musical repeat
62 Swampy areas
63 Island
64 Tinted
65 Snaky fish
66 Dorm dweller

**DOWN**

1 Meat alternative
2 Pare
3 Region
4 Given away in a drawing
5 Communicators
6 Reverent
7 Rock
8 Iraqi's neighbor
9 Sickness sign
10 Carol
11 Leer at
12 Bunches
14 Rued
20 Boundary
22 High naval rank (abbr.)
24 Extraterrestrial
25 Killed
26 Islam's head
27 Hi
28 Fake chocolate
29 Radiuses
30 Daub
33 After shower attire
35 Healing plant
40 Blonde
41 Duo
42 Mistakes
43 Wild
45 Fawn's mom
47 Eastern Standard Time
49 Drug doers
50 What a mosquito bite does
51 Thousand (abbr.)
52 Give
53 Teen hero
54 Shekel
55 Women's magazine
56 Luge
59 Caviar

| | | | | | | | | | | | |
|1|2|3|4| |5|6|7|8| |9|10|11|12|

*(crossword grid)*

## ACROSS

1 Tyrant
5 Wise Man
9 Frozen rain
13 Gumbo
14 Less
15 Meditation
16 Territory held in fee
17 Water retention
18 Blend
19 No fear
21 City
23 Italian currency
24 Nearly horizontal entrance
25 Systematic plan
28 Hollers
31 Praise
32 Deplete
34 Momma
36 Building addition
37 Miner's goal
38 Delaware
39 Droop
41 Cut of beef
43 Hello!

44 Ecological food chain (2 wds.)
46 Re-employ
48 Courts
49 __ Minor (Little Dipper)
50 What a mosquito bite does
53 Different forms of elements
57 Biblical "you"
58 Sort
60 Narrate
61 Musical repeat
62 Swampy areas
63 Island
64 Tinted
65 Snaky fish
66 Dorm dweller

## DOWN

1 Meat alternative
2 Pare
3 Region
4 Given away in a drawing
5 Communicators
6 Reverent

7 Rock
8 Iraqi's neighbor
9 Sickness sign
10 Carol
11 Leer at
12 Bunches
14 Rued
20 Boundary
22 High naval rank (abbr.)
24 Extraterrestrial
25 Killed
26 Islam's head
27 Hi
28 Fake chocolate
29 Radiuses
30 Daub
33 After shower attire
35 Healing plant
40 Blonde
41 Duo
42 Mistakes
43 Wild
45 Fawn's mom
47 Eastern Standard Time
49 Drug doers
50 What a mosquito bite does
51 Thousand (abbr.)
52 Give
53 Teen hero
54 Shekel
55 Women's magazine
56 Luge
59 Caviar

**ACROSS**

1 Black bird
5 Branch of learning
9 Clean
13 Mr. Downs of 60 minutes
14 Scorn
15 S.A. Indian
16 Island
17 Oldest
18 Drift
19 Cereal type
21 Brokers
23 Stroke
24 Tinge
25 Shape
28 Oven mitts (2 wds.)
31 Casing
32 Former wounds
34 Peter, for short
36 Miner's goal
37 Whack
38 Headed
39 Part of a semester
41 Easily taken advantage of
43 African country
44 Giant wave
46 Delicately
48 Nip
49 One time
50 Batter
53 Upsets (2 wds.)
57 Seep
58 Wrathful
60 Carved Polynesian pendant
61 Heavenly light
62 Nook
63 Native ruler
64 Standard golf scores
65 Leaves
66 Nick

**DOWN**

1 Modish
2 Spate
3 Leer at
4 Cajole
5 Dispense
6 Poles
7 Day of the wk.
8 Sounds
9 Bug
10 Soon
11 Get out!
12 Pork servings
14 Mock attacks
20 Rive
22 Gross national product (abbr.)
24 Crimes
25 Scotsman
26 Insertion mark
27 Drug doers
28 Island
29 Headquarters of British India
30 Thieve
33 Chew
35 Whirl
40 Gathers strength
41 Arranging sets
42 Mr. Doodle
43 Crowned
45 Compass point
47 Sorbet
49 Curses
50 Hospital (abbr.)
51 Small particle
52 Tyrant
53 Spice
54 Silent actor
55 Related
56 Mud
59 River (Spanish)

10 Move through the water
11 Action word
12 President (abbr.)
14 Cyclicity
20 Haunch
22 Egg layer
24 Dales
25 Paco's friend
26 Declare
27 Mails
28 One's place
29 Moral principles
30 Household insect
33 Ancient Indian
35 Parent groups
40 Staff
41 Leafy green
42 Warming device
43 Study of poetry
45 Be
47 Pounds per square inch
49 Weight unit
50 Leaky faucet noise
51 Helper
52 Weight unit
53 Legal claim to property
54 Ca. University
55 Believe
56 Bezel
59 ___ shot (2 wds.)

## ACROSS

1 A spinning toy (2 wds.)
5 Open tart-like pastry
9 Invitation abbreviaton
13 Sego lily's bulb
14 Produce
15 Vessel
16 Snaky fish
17 Shells
18 Shoot
19 Purple quartz
21 Short fingers
23 Baseball glove
24 Dale
25 Mary's husband
28 Svelte
31 Ajar
32 Paired sock
34 Finish
36 Transgression
37 Type of Buddhism
38 Shake
39 Ceases
41 Hide away
43 Typesetting
   measurement
44 Free
46 Time periods
48 Little Mermaid's love
49 Casing
50 Make softer
53 Not longitude
57 Mob activity
58 Ablaze
60 Chilled
61 Bored
62 Limpid
63 Fly
64 Look
65 Go after
66 Identical

## DOWN

1 At sea
2 Seethe
3 Leer at
4 Mailmen
5 Book by Goethe
6 Gait
7 American sign language
8 Snuggled
9 Rebates

## Crossword Grid

A crossword puzzle grid with numbered cells (1–66).

## ACROSS

1 Challenging
5 Small licorice treats
9 Dart
13 Assure
14 Ross ___, philanthropist
15 Do it again
16 National capital
17 Spiky
18 Capital of Norway
19 On other side of ocean
21 Beam
23 Out of bounds
24 River dirt
25 Pique
28 Bring into bondage
31 Pushy
32 Vegetable
34 Clean
36 Roberto's yes
37 Hubbub
38 Rest
39 Paradise
41 Piousness
43 Bona ___
44 Astral
46 Worn
48 Ornament
49 Become less distinct
50 South-Central Dravidian
53 Wire
57 Spoken
58 Funeral hymn
60 European monetary unit
61 Flat bread
62 Colder
63 Tyrant
64 Oracle
65 Written material
66 Southeast by east

## DOWN

1 Angel's head ring
2 Tel ___
3 Capital of Italy
4 Overshadowed
5 Asian country
6 Part of the eye
7 ___ fire
8 Spruce
9 ___ lobe, front brain section
10 For fear that
11 Bored
12 Working implement
14 Fake
20 Child
22 Ailing
24 Schnozzle
25 Band instrument
26 Bends
27 Swift
28 Bedspread feather
29 Legal
30 Keep away from
33 Mythological water nymph
35 Looked
40 Gas like cloud
41 Enthusiastic approval
42 Old ___ (TV dog)
43 Misses
45 Limb
47 Regret
49 Father
50 Not bottom
51 Canal
52 Tardy
53 Kid's cereal brand
54 Tactic
55 Middle East dweller
56 Extra
59 Sorbet

**ACROSS**

1 Exchange
5 Imitated
9 Sharpen by rubbing
13 Helper
14 Sound of a sneeze
15 European monetary unit
16 Male deer
17 Card game
18 Opera solo
19 Grenade shard
21 Plowed
23 Told
24 Tinge
25 Pillar
28 Pounded
31 Famous cookies
32 On your way
34 365 days
36 Newspaper
37 Pod vegetable
38 River (Spanish)
39 Ruined
41 Salaam
43 River dirt
44 Butt destination
46 Bowling __
48 Plush
49 Leg joint
50 Crank
53 Similarity
57 Sculls
58 Wrathful
60 Traced
61 A wager (2 wds.)
62 Dubbed
63 Austin novel
64 Hotel furniture
65 Compass point
66 Shower

**DOWN**

1 Talk back
2 Along
3 6th month (Jewish calendar)
4 Winged horse
5 Was sore
6 Mr. Donahue
7 Aurora
8 Dabbing
9 Rich
10 Lunge
11 Canal
12 Frog's cousin
14 Canopy
20 Brand of non-stick spray
22 Business abbr.
24 Canned meats
25 Autos
26 City
27 Company symbols
28 Piousness
29 Spooky
30 Newspaper frequency
33 Ms. Winfrey
35 Decays
40 Lunges
41 Gamins
42 Tugged
43 Svelte
45 Twitching
47 Downwind
49 Wind toys
50 Wrest
51 Kimono
52 Unpaid
53 Mutton
54 Writer Bombeck
55 Partial
56 Cob
59 Underdone

**ACROSS**

1 Exchange
5 Imitated
9 Sharpen by rubbing
13 Helper
14 Sound of a sneeze
15 European monetary unit
16 Male deer
17 Card game
18 Opera solo
19 Grenade shard
21 Plowed
23 Told
24 Tinge
25 Pillar
28 Pounded
31 Famous cookies
32 On your way
34 365 days
36 Newspaper
37 Pod vegetable
38 River (Spanish)
39 Ruined
41 Salaam
43 River dirt
44 Butt destination

46 Bowling __
48 Plush
49 Leg joint
50 Crank
53 Similarity
57 Sculls
58 Wrathful
60 Traced
61 A wager (2 wds.)
62 Dubbed
63 Austin novel
64 Hotel furniture
65 Compass point
66 Shower

**DOWN**

1 Talk back
2 Along
3 6th month (Jewish calendar)
4 Winged horse
5 Was sore
6 Mr. Donahue
7 Aurora
8 Dabbing
9 Rich

10 Lunge
11 Canal
12 Frog's cousin
14 Canopy
20 Brand of non-stick spray
22 Business abbr.
24 Canned meats
25 Autos
26 City
27 Company symbols
28 Piousness
29 Spooky
30 Newspaper frequency
33 Ms. Winfrey
35 Decays
40 Lunges
41 Gamins
42 Tugged
43 Svelte
45 Twitching
47 Downwind
49 Wind toys
50 Wrest
51 Kimono
52 Unpaid
53 Mutton
54 Writer Bombeck
55 Partial
56 Cob
59 Underdone

**ACROSS**

1 Southeast by east
5 Glen
9 Preparation (abbr.)
13 Wind
14 Forest god
15 Midwestern state
16 Put on __
17 Finned mammal
18 Sulk
19 Highest N. American Mt.
21 Changes a text
23 Superman's Ms. Lane
24 Upon
25 One of the bases
28 Confused
31 Soon
32 Thin flat strips
34 Pig
36 Spanish "one"
37 Wrath
38 Miner's goal
39 N.T. book
41 Inactive
43 Capital of Western Samoa
44 Isles
46 Consequence
48 Region
49 Interbreeding population within a species
50 Displayer of emotions
53 Cottage
57 Indonesian island
58 Sport groups
60 Strong cord
61 Dunking cookies
62 Type of wood
63 Fencing sword
64 Lighted sign
65 Totals
66 Decorate

**DOWN**

1 Played in the water
2 Little Mermaid's love
3 Tree covering
4 5th Greek letter
5 Courts
6 Attorney (abbr.)
7 Caustic substance
8 Somethings to run
9 Small-arms
10 Memorization
11 Vessel
12 Animal hands
14 Opposite of liquids
20 Not (refix)
22 Limited (abbr.)
24 Outside layer
25 Paul's former name
26 Boredom
27 Roasts
28 Ticket costs
29 Marry secretly
30 Not ionic
33 Singer Ronstadt
35 Batter
40 Excitement
41 Physics motion tendency
42 Little
43 Afraid
45 Be
47 Madagascar franc (abbr.)
49 French author
50 Black
51 Foal's mom
52 Tub spread
53 Hairless
54 Run easily
55 Organization of Petroleum Exporting Countries
56 Seven days
59 Abort

**ACROSS**

1 Pituitary hormone
5 Not many (2 wds.)
9 Cast off
13 Scat!
14 God of Islam
15 Well
16 Royalty
17 National capital
18 Judge
19 Relic
21 Berated
23 Wharf
24 Otherwise
25 Hunting expedition
28 Journeyed
31 Member of an alliance
32 Uttered
34 Frozen rain
36 Thai
37 New York City
38 Grain
39 Volcano
41 Desires
43 Count votes
44 Yolk (2 wds.)

46 Combined
48 Love flower
49 Saturates
50 One of the N. and S. States
53 AKA Scotchman
57 Organization concerned with civil liberties (abbr.)
58 Meal
60 Relive
61 Persia
62 Taboos
63 Skier's need
64 Mail
65 Paradise
66 Oceans

**DOWN**

1 At sea
2 Blacken
3 Wrongdoing
4 No work day
5 Expression of regret
6 Dart
7 Hearing part
8 Looped

9 Screams
10 Draw
11 Women's magazine
12 Accomplishment
14 Gum arabic
20 Pro
22 Request
24 Construct
25 Satiate
26 Having wings
27 Spree
28 Rendezvous
29 Enter
30 Creator of Sherlock Holmes
33 Make used to
35 Join metal
40 On the shore
41 Italian dish
42 Dishes out
43 Have
45 Pan's partner
47 Choose
49 Plant shoot
50 Pulpit
51 Land measurement
52 Part of the "KKK"
53 Reasonable
54 Cause
55 Land mass
56 Loch __ monster
59 Pole

## Crossword Grid

(Grid 14×14 with numbered cells: 1–66)

## Clues

### ACROSS

1 Stain
5 Compass point
9 Animal insect
13 National capital
14 Dismay
15 Prevaricator
16 Swerve
17 Small amount
18 Niche
19 Denim work trouser
21 Carsickness symptom queasiness
23 Eager
24 September (abbr.)
25 Surroundings
28 Joy
31 Persia
32 Business mail
34 Scotsman
36 Zip
37 Cut grass
38 Possessive pronoun
39 Island
41 Damply
43 Sand pile
44 Cleanliness
46 Surface
48 High School senior
49 Jester
50 Goal maker
53 Metal urns with spigots
57 Tropical edible root
58 Musical production
60 Teen hero
61 Opaque gem
62 Not rural
63 Treaty organization
64 Cured
65 Has toed
66 Planted

### DOWN

1 Ave.'s opposite
2 In __ of
3 Bode
4 Barter
5 Fastness
6 Fencing sword
7 Disallow
8 Guile
9 Mexican deep fried food
10 Mouth parts
11 Relive
12 Region
14 Roman's courtyard
20 Avenue
22 Liable
24 Frown
25 Short
26 UK members
27 Not strictly
28 Show emotions
29 Scrub
30 Baby, for example
33 Improve
35 Elm
40 Won ton companion (2 wds.)
41 Tire (2 wds.)
42 Navy cleric
43 Digging into
45 Wrath
47 Cow sound
49 Unit of electric capacitance
50 Store
51 Point
52 Spoken
53 Southeast by east
54 6th month (Jewish calendar)
55 Memorization
56 Not fast
59 For

**ACROSS**

1 Leave undone
5 Asian dress
9 Rodent
13 "as you __"
14 Edge stitch
15 Belief
16 Cereal ingredient
17 Ancient Indian
18 Gal
19 Canadian city
21 Student lodging
23 University (abbr.)
24 Redneck
25 Bogus
28 ___ Sunfire
31 Fallen
32 Amid
34 Invalidated
36 Expression of surprise
37 Gall
38 Stamping tool
39 Join
41 In the ___, person
43 National capital
44 Tasted

46 Spoke
48 Positive
49 Pixies
50 School writings
53 Draws
57 Sports event
58 Actor Paul (of Crocodile Dundee)
60 Wind
61 Speed
62 Type of wood
63 African river
64 Chichi
65 Cosecant's opposite
66 Brews

**DOWN**

1 Compass point
2 Lotion brand
3 Persia
4 Team flag
5 Looked over, with "up"
6 Acting (abbr.)
7 Caviar
8 Scratching
9 Football

10 Blue-pencil
11 Ecological communities
12 Lanky
14 Tropical fruit
20 Sorbet
22 Fall mo.
24 Beeps like a car
25 Fun
26 Hostess creation
27 Japanese city
28 Read over
29 Tax payer's fear
30 Climate
33 __ per hour
35 Poisonous metal
40 Emotional understanding
41 Turns red
42 Processed corn
43 Italian dish
45 Wooden sheet
47 Revolutions per minute
49 Silly
50 Austin novel
51 Scorch
52 Clique
53 Competition at the Greek games
54 Animal's end part
55 Women's magazine
56 Perceives with eye
59 Kimono sash

**ACROSS**

1 Interbreeding population within a species
5 What children learn
9 Bullets
13 Cruel
14 Select
15 Rich dirt
16 Plateau
17 White, powdery substance
18 S.A. Indian
19 Exhilarate
21 Arouse
23 Replace a striker
24 Chest bones
25 Cash in
28 14 line poems
31 Old
32 Folklore tales
34 Dinner table seasoning
36 Short-term memory
37 Writing liquid
38 Murmur
39 Inheritor
41 Potter's needs
43 Brad ___, actor
44 Response getters
46 Material
48 Move past
49 Work
50 Facet
53 Disappointments
57 Adam's son
58 Terminate
60 Tack
61 Elm
62 Comfortable
63 Not out of
64 Encircle
65 Chewy candies
66 Sulk

**DOWN**

1 Prefix for half
2 Tied
3 Feel the lack of
4 Slipped by
5 Improvise a speech
6 Buskin
7 Central processing unit
8 Stresses
9 False names
10 Friar
11 Spice
12 Asian country
14 "A" shaped house (2 wds.)
20 Sorbet
22 West by north
24 Poor relationship
25 Spate
26 Painter Richard
27 Resign
28 Moses' mountain
29 Unexpressed
30 Slow tree mammal
33 Medicine doses
35 Children
40 Matured
41 Pudding-like dessert
42 Scottish terriers
43 Near celestial pole
45 IBM Competitor
47 Liberal (abbr.)
49 What is agreed upon
50 Acting (abbr.)
51 Asian dress
52 Jetty
53 Chimney dirt
54 Penny
55 Soaring plaything
56 Frozen rain
59 Condemn

**ACROSS**

1 Peddle
5 Lager
9 Otherwise
13 Buckeye State
14 Sleep disorder
15 Brook
16 Shekel
17 What a vending machine takes
18 Spoken
19 Tacit
21 Bun topping seed
23 Cain killed him
24 Carved Polynesian pendant
25 Requests
28 Ancient Assyria capital
31 Piece of land
32 Canned chili brand
34 Shine
36 Eye infection
37 Fire remains
38 Women's undergarment
39 Citizen
41 Anger
43 Toot
44 Draw into a tangle
46 Honors
48 Merely
49 Cruel
50 What bee's distribute
53 Docile
57 Region
58 Unfasten the pins of
60 Opp. of yeses
61 Chair
62 Works
63 Thunder __
64 Tint
65 Wobble
66 Whirl

**DOWN**

1 N.A. Indian
2 Excuse me!
3 Thin strand
4 Drink mix brand
5 Plunder
6 Part
7 Thief's hideout
8 Talking back
9 Wears down
10 Italian currency
11 Close the door hard
12 Women's magazine
14 Get at
20 Large computer co.
22 Stretch to make do
24 Opp. of loose
25 Saclike structures filled with fluid or diseased matter
26 Woodworker's tool
27 White
28 Whining speech
29 Fire remains
30 Leased
33 Hang around
35 Raps lightly
40 Place alone
41 Hard shelled nuts
42 Harbors
43 Stabilize
45 Compass point
47 Beat
49 Author Dickinson
50 Yore
51 Dunking cookies
52 Lanky
53 Capital of Western Samoa
54 Pushy
55 Poisonous metal
56 Spot
59 This time

## ACROSS

1 African country
5 Keats
9 Moved air
13 Toboggan
14 Crooked
15 Not mine
16 Winged
17 Monte __
18 Telegram
19 Satellite dish shape
21 Fall
23 "Cheers" regular
24 Huge whale
25 Saying
28 Emblems
31 Greek goddess of youth
32 Slippery rock
34 Sense
36 Dined
37 Also known as (abbr.)
38 Deuce
39 Gents
41 Salesperson
43 Gets older
44 Freaks

46 Slight
48 Baths
49 Male deer
50 Festive
53 Abated
57 Hurt
58 Abraham's son
60 Do it again
61 Not us
62 Refined
63 Canal
64 Turfs
65 Ceases
66 Chewy candies

## DOWN

1 Thunder __
2 __ hoop (child's toy)
3 Seaweed substance
4 Unsettle
5 Sacred poem
6 Gumbo
7 Elver
8 Duo
9 Via (3 wds.)
10 Superman's Ms. Lane

11 European monetary unit
12 Small bird
14 Nuts
20 Snake
22 Move away
24 Shiny balloon material
25 Thick carpet
26 Rest
27 Does what their told
28 For one's good
29 Unhand (2 wds.)
30 Needle worker
33 Auras
35 Mislay
40 Methods
41 Goblet
42 Trite artwork
43 Galled
45 Accountant
47 Ozone
49 Couches
50 Oils
51 Reverberate
52 Cast off
53 Praise
54 Roman emperor
55 Blue-pencil
56 Did
59 Child

**11** Abundant
**12** Extremely long time periods
**14** Cry-baby
**20** Klutz
**22** Record
**24** Longitudinal
**25** Eye infection
**26** Profession
**27** Refund
**28** Jostle
**29** Musical tones
**30** Chest
**33** Enter
**35** Baseball's Nolan
**40** Series of songs
**41** Hauler
**42** Exacts
**43** Archive incorrectly
**45** Stinger
**47** Stamping tool
**49** Jargon
**50** Sinks
**51** Capital of Norway
**52** Elated
**53** Annoys
**54** Teen hero
**55** Loch __ monster
**56** Fence opening
**59** Maturity

## ACROSS

**1** Rotate
**5** Charity
**9** Scarce
**13** Had on, as clothing
**14** Carry off
**15** Native ruler
**16** Tell
**17** Fence of bushes
**18** Settee
**19** Giant trees
**21** Advantages
**23** Touch down
**24** Particle
**25** Shoot from a plane
**28** Taxing
**31** Elm
**32** Antiquity
**34** Entry
**36** Talk incessantly
**37** BB association
**38** Sample
**39** Cheese
**41** Humorous
**43** Plateau
**44** Facial hair arch

**46** Phonograph inventor
**48** Do business
**49** Car rental agency
**50** Sharp angled path
**53** Supplying information
**57** Island
**58** Measuring device
**60** Belief
**61** Fun
**62** Kellogg's waffles
**63** Fallen
**64** Turfs
**65** Lay
**66** Otherwise

## DOWN

**1** Compass point
**2** Geographical points
**3** Asian country
**4** Interstellar gases
**5** In the lead
**6** Caps
**7** Chinese seasoning
**8** Doubter
**9** Began again
**10** Famous cookies

**Solution:**

| A | D | H | D | | | U | T | A | H |
|---|---|---|---|---|---|---|---|---|---|
| L | I | A | R | | P | R | I | M | A |
| E | R | I | E | | I | N | L | A | Y |
| S | T | R | A | W | S | | D | I | E |
| | | | D | I | C | K | E | N | S |
| O | A | R | S | M | E | N | | | |
| P | R | O | | P | S | A | L | M | S |
| R | E | B | E | L | | V | I | O | L |
| A | N | I | L | E | | E | L | L | E |
| H | A | N | K | | | S | T | E | W |

**Solution:**

| E | B | B | S | | | G | E | R | M |
|---|---|---|---|---|---|---|---|---|---|
| C | L | O | P | | A | N | J | O | U |
| H | O | S | E | | S | P | E | N | T |
| O | B | S | E | S | S | | C | D | T |
| | | | | C | H | E | E | T | O | S |
| H | I | G | H | E | S | T | | | |
| A | T | E | | | A | S | Y | L | U | M |
| R | A | T | E | R | | M | I | N | E |
| P | L | O | T | S | | O | M | I | T |
| S | Y | N | C | | | N | O | T | E |

**Solution:**

| O | D | O | R |   |   |   | H | I | F | I |
| P | A | P | A |   |   | B | O | N | E | D |
| E | T | U | I |   |   | H | E | N | R | I |
| N | A | S | S | A | U |   | E | G | O |   |
|   |   |   |   | I | N | T | E | R | I | M |
| G | R | A | N | D | A | M |   |   |   |   |
| H | A | D |   | E | N | I | G | M | A |   |
| O | M | A | H | A |   | G | R | U | B |   |
| S | I | M | O | N |   | R | A | T | E |   |
| T | E | S | T |   |   |   | E | Y | E | D |

**Solution:**

| C | O | M | A | | | D | A | T | A |
| A | R | I | D | | C | U | M | I | N |
| L | E | N | O | | A | D | U | L | T |
| M | O | N | R | O | E | | S | E | E |
| | | | | E | X | C | E | E | D | S |
| F | E | A | R | F | U | L | | | |
| E | G | G | | O | M | E | L | E | T |
| T | Y | L | E | R | | C | U | T | E |
| U | P | E | N | D | | T | R | U | E |
| S | T | Y | E | | | S | K | I | N |

**Solution:**

| E | B | B | S | | | | P | L | E | A |
| M | A | R | C | | | S | T | I | N | K |
| U | T | A | H | | | P | A | S | T | E |
| S | E | N | E | C | A | | L | E | E |
| | | | | M | I | D | T | E | R | M |
| P | A | N | A | C | E | A | | | |
| A | G | O | | A | S | S | I | S | T |
| S | A | L | A | D | | T | S | A | R |
| T | I | A | R | A | | E | L | L | E |
| A | N | N | E | | | S | E | E | K |

**Solution:**

| W | A | Y | S | | | O | S | L | O |
|---|---|---|---|---|---|---|---|---|---|
| A | R | E | A | | B | A | Y | O | U |
| S | I | L | T | | A | K | R | O | N |
| P | A | P | Y | R | I | | I | N | C |
| | | | | R | E | L | E | A | S | E |
| D | R | E | S | D | E | N | | | |
| O | I | L | | G | R | A | Z | E | D |
| O | V | U | L | E | | C | E | D | E |
| M | A | D | A | M | | T | R | A | M |
| S | L | E | W | | S | O | M | E | |

**Solution:**

| | | | | | | | | | |
|---|---|---|---|---|---|---|---|---|---|
| C | H | E | F | ■ | ■ | S | L | U | E |
| H | U | R | L | ■ | P | R | I | N | T |
| A | S | I | A | ■ | H | I | N | D | U |
| P | H | E | N | O | L | ■ | D | I | D |
| ■ | ■ | ■ | G | R | E | N | A | D | E |
| R | E | V | E | N | G | E | ■ | ■ | ■ |
| A | L | I | ■ | E | M | E | R | G | E |
| P | A | R | E | R | ■ | D | A | R | D |
| I | T | A | L | Y | ■ | E | T | U | I |
| D | E | L | L | ■ | ■ | D | E | B | T |

**Solution:**

| T | S | A | R |   |   | E | A | T | S |
|---|---|---|---|---|---|---|---|---|---|
| H | Y | P | E |   | M | Y | R | R | H |
| A | L | E | S |   | A | E | R | I | E |
| T | I | D | I | E | R |   | A | C | E |
|   |   |   |   | D | E | L | A | Y | E | R |
| I | N | T | E | R | I | M |   |   |   |
| S | A | Y |   | I | N | U | R | E | D |
| A | P | P | A | L |   | L | U | G | E |
| A | P | E | R | Y |   | E | B | O | N |
| C | Y | S | T |   |   | T | E | S | T |

**Solution:**

| S | L | I | M |   |   | S | I | L | O |
|---|---|---|---|---|---|---|---|---|---|
| P | E | R | U |   | H | A | V | O | C |
| A | N | O | N |   | U | N | I | T | E |
| M | O | N | I | S | M |   | E | T | A |
|   |   |   |   | C | H | A | N | S | O | N |
| A | F | G | H | A | N | I |   |   |   |
| E | E | L |   | S | E | A | M | A | N |
| G | I | A | N | T |   | C | A | F | E |
| I | N | D | I | A |   | I | D | E | A |
| S | T | E | P |   |   | N | E | W | T |

**Solution:**

| C | Z | A | R |   |   | P | E | C | S |
|---|---|---|---|---|---|---|---|---|---|
| R | I | C | H |   | H | A | V | O | C |
| A | T | T | Y |   | O | S | A | K | A |
| B | I | S | T | R | O |   | D | E | N |
|   |   |   |   | H | A | P | L | E | S | S |
| T | R | A | M | P | L | E |   |   |   |
| H | U | B |   | P | A | N | D | A | S |
| I | R | A | T | E |   | T | U | B | E |
| E | A | S | E | D |   | I | N | C | A |
| F | L | E | A |   |   | L | E | S | S |

**Solution:**

| B | E | M | A |   |   | A | L | S | O |
|---|---|---|---|---|---|---|---|---|---|
| O | R | A | L |   | B | R | I | E | F |
| A | I | R | S |   | R | E | M | I | T |
| T | E | X | A | C | O |   | E | N | E |
|   |   |   |   | C | O | A | R | S | E | N |
| S | C | I | E | N | C | E |   |   |   |
| W | A | C |   | S | H | R | A | N | K |
| A | D | I | E | U |   | E | B | O | N |
| P | R | E | L | L |   | A | L | O | E |
| S | E | R | F |   |   | D | Y | K | E |

**Solution:**

| A | B | B | A |   |   | B | A | S | E |
| L | U | L | L |   | P | O | U | N | D |
| S | N | U | B |   | S | P | R | I | G |
| O | K | E | E | F | E |   | A | P | E |
|   |   |   |   | D | O | U | B | L | E | S |
| L | A | S | O | R | D | A |   |   |   |
| I | C | E |   | M | O | S | T | L | Y |
| L | U | N | G | E |   | S | H | O | E |
| A | R | D | O | R |   | E | A | R | L |
| C | A | S | T |   |   | S | T | E | P |

**Solution:**

| S | N | O | B | | | H | E | M | P |
| Y | O | R | E | | D | I | D | O | S |
| L | O | B | E | | A | M | E | B | A |
| I | N | S | T | E | P | | M | I | L |
| | | | L | I | P | B | A | L | M |
| Q | U | I | E | T | L | Y | | | |
| U | R | N | | H | E | L | P | E | D |
| A | B | U | S | E | | I | O | T | A |
| R | A | R | E | R | | N | O | U | N |
| K | N | E | W | | | E | R | I | E |

**Solution:**

| S | P | A | S |   |   |   | A | G | E | S |   |   | A | M | E | N |
|---|---|---|---|---|---|---|---|---|---|---|---|---|---|---|---|---|
| H | U | L | A |   |   | T | I | L | A | K |   |   | R | I | D | E |
| O | R | A | L |   |   | E | R | A | S | E |   |   | S | N | I | T |
| T | E | R | E | S | A |   | D | E | T | R | O | I | T |   |   |   |
|   |   |   | M | E | S | A |   | S | C | A | N |   |   |   |   |   |
| A | F | C |   | P | E | L | T |   | H | Y | I | N | G |   |   |   |
| B | O | O |   | A | L | L | O | W |   |   | S | O | L | D |   |   |
| B | R | A | W | L |   | E | T | A |   | U | T | T | E | R |   |   |
| A | U | T | O |   |   | N | A | D | I | R |   | E | N | E |   |   |
|   | M | I | N | O | R |   | L | I | M | B |   | S | S | W |   |   |
|   |   | D | A | I | S |   | S | P | A | T |   |   |   |   |   |   |
|   | N | A | R | R | O | W | S |   | U | N | E | S | C | O |   |   |
| L | O | C | O |   | T | E | N | O | R |   | S | T | O | W |   |   |
| O | A | H | U |   | E | D | U | C | E |   | T | O | T | E |   |   |
| W | H | Y | S |   | D | E | B | T |   |   | S | P | E | D |   |   |

**Solution:**

| S | O | R | T | ■ | ■ | C | N | S | ■ | ■ | A | F | A | R |
|---|---|---|---|---|---|---|---|---|---|---|---|---|---|---|
| A | P | I | A | ■ | T | H | A | I | S | ■ | M | I | C | E |
| D | E | C | K | ■ | Z | E | B | R | A | ■ | A | J | A | X |
| ■ | C | A | E | S | A | R | ■ | E | U | C | L | I | D | ■ |
| ■ | S | H | R | U | B | ■ | L | U | G | ■ | | | | |
| A | S | C | I | I | ■ | B | I | C | ■ | T | A | B | B | Y |
| T | W | I | N | E | D | ■ | K | P | H | ■ | M | A | L | E |
| T | A | R | ■ | D | E | V | I | S | E | D | ■ | B | U | N |
| I | T | C | H | ■ | C | A | N | ■ | R | O | B | E | R | T |
| C | H | A | O | S | ■ | T | I | C | ■ | M | A | L | T | A |
| ■ | R | O | E | ■ | S | A | W | E | D | ■ | | | | |
| ■ | C | A | R | T | E | L | ■ | M | I | D | G | E | T | |
| F | O | C | I | ■ | L | I | B | E | L | ■ | E | R | I | C |
| C | O | I | F | ■ | S | L | Y | L | Y | ■ | R | I | N | D |
| A | N | D | Y | ■ | Y | E | S | ■ | S | E | E | S | | |

**Solution:**

| E | P | E | E | ■ | ■ | M | A | R | C | ■ | P | R | O | S |
| B | O | D | Y | ■ | H | U | M | P | H | ■ | L | E | N | T |
| B | R | I | E | ■ | A | R | O | M | A | ■ | A | N | T | I |
| S | E | T | B | A | C | K | S | ■ | L | E | C | T | O | R |
| ■ | ■ | ■ | A | L | K | Y | ■ | P | E | T | E | ■ | ■ | ■ |
| G | R | I | L | L | E | ■ | M | U | T | A | B | L | E | ■ |
| E | A | R | L | ■ | R | O | A | R | S | ■ | O | I | L | S |
| A | G | O | ■ | ■ | U | T | E | ■ | ■ | ■ | V | I | A | ■ |
| R | E | N | D | ■ | U | T | T | E | R | ■ | K | I | D | S |
| ■ | S | Y | R | I | N | G | E | ■ | A | S | I | D | E | S |
| ■ | ■ | O | L | E | O | ■ | S | C | U | D | ■ | ■ | ■ | ■ |
| C | A | N | O | L | A | ■ | S | C | I | E | N | C | E | S |
| H | E | A | P | ■ | R | I | P | E | N | ■ | A | L | T | O |
| E | R | I | E | ■ | T | W | A | N | G | ■ | P | O | U | R |
| F | O | L | D | ■ | H | O | N | E | ■ | ■ | S | P | I | T |

**Solution:**

| S | P | A | N | ■ | ■ | O | W | E | D | ■ | A | B | B | R |
|---|---|---|---|---|---|---|---|---|---|---|---|---|---|---|
| N | O | N | O | ■ | A | D | I | E | U | ■ | M | A | L | I |
| A | U | T | O | ■ | C | O | N | G | A | ■ | B | L | O | B |
| G | R | I | N | D | E | R | S | ■ | L | Y | R | I | C | S |
| ■ | ■ | D | A | D | S | ■ | V | I | I | I | ■ | ■ | ■ | ■ |
| S | A | L | A | M | I | ■ | D | I | S | P | E | L | S | ■ |
| C | L | O | Y | ■ | A | L | A | R | M | ■ | S | O | A | R |
| O | L | D | ■ | ■ | A | U | G | ■ | ■ | R | U | E |   |   |
| T | O | G | O | P | I | N | O | N | ■ | L | A | N | D |   |
| ■ | W | E | T | D | I | R | T | ■ | A | R | E | N | A | S |
| ■ | ■ | T | E | A | S | ■ | C | R | A | G | ■ | ■ |   |   |
| D | I | S | O | W | N | ■ | B | O | R | D | E | R | E | D |
| A | D | A | M | ■ | I | D | A | H | O | ■ | N | I | L | E |
| T | O | G | A | ■ | S | I | N | E | W | ■ | D | O | S | E |
| E | L | A | N | ■ | T | E | E | N | ■ | S | T | E | P |   |

**Solution:**

| M | A | P | S | | | S | A | Y | S | | | H | A | T | E |
| A | C | L | U | | | O | P | R | A | H | | O | D | O | R |
| T | R | O | D | | | H | A | I | K | U | | M | A | M | A |
| H | E | P | A | T | I | C | A | | | C | R | I | M | E | S |
| | | | | F | L | O | E | | | A | K | I | N | | |
| S | E | N | E | C | A | | | S | W | E | D | I | S | H | |
| P | A | I | D | | | N | A | I | A | D | | D | E | A | D |
| U | S | E | | | | P | S | I | | | | | O | U | R |
| D | E | C | A | | | V | I | S | T | A | | T | U | N | A |
| | L | E | P | R | O | S | Y | | R | E | A | L | T | Y | |
| | | | | P | I | T | H | | L | I | S | P | | | |
| C | H | A | R | G | E | | V | I | S | C | E | R | A | L | |
| Y | O | G | I | | S | P | O | R | E | | R | A | V | E | |
| S | P | A | S | | I | O | W | A | N | | E | G | I | S | |
| T | I | R | E | | N | E | S | S | | | D | U | S | T | |

**Solution:**

| C | A | M | P | | | S | O | F | A | | P | U | G | S |
|---|---|---|---|---|---|---|---|---|---|---|---|---|---|---|
| O | B | O | E | | H | I | N | D | U | | A | T | O | P |
| M | U | O | N | | A | T | L | A | S | | R | A | G | E |
| A | T | T | O | R | N | E | Y | | T | V | S | H | O | W |
| | | | C | U | S | S | | P | E | E | L | | | |
| T | O | W | H | E | E | | B | A | R | T | E | N | D | |
| A | P | I | A | | L | A | R | G | E | | Y | O | U | R |
| L | I | D | | | B | O | A | | | | | T | E | A |
| K | N | E | E | | B | L | O | N | D | | K | E | L | P |
| | E | N | T | E | R | E | D | | A | M | I | D | S | T |
| | | H | E | I | R | | D | I | R | T | | | | |
| A | S | S | I | G | N | | P | E | N | S | T | O | C | K |
| C | H | I | C | | G | R | E | E | T | | I | R | A | N |
| C | O | L | A | | T | A | R | D | Y | | E | A | S | E |
| T | O | O | L | | O | P | U | S | | | S | L | E | W |

**Solution:**

| S | T | O | P |   |   | E | C | H | O |   | F | I | F | O |
| Y | O | R | E |   | S | Q | U | A | B |   | I | R | O | N |
| L | I | A | R |   | M | U | T | T | S |   | R | A | I | L |
| I | L | L | I | N | O | I | S |   | E | V | E | N | L | Y |
|   |   |   | L | O | O | P |   | A | R | I | D |   |   |   |
| A | S | S | E | R | T |   | E | N | V | I | O | U | S |   |
| C | H | A | D |   | H | I | N | G | E |   | G | R | U | B |
| E | E | L |   |   |   | C | A | L |   |   |   | G | E | E |
| S | A | V | E |   | N | I | C | E | R |   | C | E | D | E |
|   | F | O | X | H | U | N | T |   | E | R | A | S | E | S |
|   |   | T | A | N | G |   | W | A | Y | S |   |   |   |   |
| S | O | L | E | M | N |   | S | I | D | E | S | T | E | P |
| W | H | E | N |   | E | R | A | S | E |   | A | R | E | A |
| B | I | N | D |   | R | O | G | E | R |   | T | I | L | L |
| S | O | D | S |   | Y | E | A | R |   |   | T | O | S | S |

**Solution:**

| C | A | T | S | ■ | ■ | W | A | C | S | ■ | R | I | S | E |
|---|---|---|---|---|---|---|---|---|---|---|---|---|---|---|
| H | E | R | E | ■ | A | A | N | D | W | ■ | O | B | E | Y |
| E | R | I | E | ■ | P | I | N | T | O | ■ | T | I | R | E |
| F | O | O | T | N | O | T | E | ■ | O | P | U | S | E | S |
| ■ | ■ | ■ | ■ | H | O | G | S | ■ | S | P | A | N | ■ | ■ |
| A | C | C | E | D | E | ■ | W | I | E | L | D | E | D | ■ |
| C | L | O | D | ■ | E | M | E | N | D | ■ | A | X | O | N |
| L | A | P | ■ | ■ | ■ | C | I | A | ■ | ■ | ■ | C | W | O |
| U | S | S | R | ■ | A | C | R | I | D | ■ | K | E | E | N |
| ■ | H | E | A | D | G | O | D | ■ | A | P | O | L | L | O |
| ■ | ■ | M | I | R | Y | ■ | G | N | A | W | ■ | ■ | ■ | ■ |
| V | I | R | A | G | O | ■ | H | O | I | S | T | I | N | G |
| I | C | E | D | ■ | U | S | E | R | S | ■ | O | D | O | R |
| S | O | D | A | ■ | N | E | I | G | H | ■ | W | O | V | E |
| A | N | O | N | ■ | D | A | R | E | ■ | ■ | S | L | A | Y |

**Solution:**

| P | A | W | S | | | N | A | P | E | | | P | A | G | E |
|---|---|---|---|---|---|---|---|---|---|---|---|---|---|---|---|
| T | R | A | P | | P | I | L | A | F | | | O | P | E | N |
| A | E | R | O | | S | H | E | L | F | | | L | E | N | D |
| S | A | M | U | R | A | I | S | | | A | P | E | X | E | S |
| | | | | T | O | L | L | | S | C | A | M | | | |
| E | S | T | E | E | M | | M | E | E | T | I | N | G | | |
| L | E | W | D | | S | C | A | N | S | | | C | E | L | L |
| A | G | E | | | | | I | R | S | | | | R | U | E |
| N | O | E | S | | A | S | S | E | T | | | E | V | E | N |
| | S | T | A | U | N | C | H | | | A | L | L | E | Y | S |
| | | U | N | D | O | | | F | R | E | E | | | | |
| D | O | C | T | O | R | | A | A | R | D | V | A | R | K | |
| O | G | L | E | | E | N | S | U | E | | | A | G | U | E |
| T | R | U | E | | W | I | E | L | D | | | T | O | N | Y |
| S | E | E | D | | S | L | A | T | | | | E | G | G | S |

**Solution:**

| G | Y | P | S | █ | █ | S | A | U | L | █ | R | A | S | H |
|---|---|---|---|---|---|---|---|---|---|---|---|---|---|---|
| R | O | O | T | █ | S | T | A | T | E | █ | E | R | I | E |
| A | G | U | E | █ | P | Y | R | E | X | █ | C | I | T | E |
| F | I | R | E | D | A | M | P | █ | I | S | R | A | E | L |
| █ | █ | █ | P | O | S | Y | █ | A | C | L | U | █ | █ | █ |
| H | A | R | L | E | M | █ | S | L | A | Y | I | N | G | █ |
| E | P | E | E | █ | S | E | P | A | L | █ | T | O | R | E |
| E | H | F | █ | █ | █ | S | I | R | █ | █ | █ | B | U | D |
| D | I | E | M | █ | I | T | E | M | S | █ | S | L | E | D |
| █ | D | R | U | M | M | E | D | █ | H | O | M | E | L | Y |
| █ | █ | █ | S | O | M | E | █ | D | O | D | O | █ | █ | █ |
| S | E | C | E | D | E | █ | H | U | D | D | L | I | N | G |
| O | A | H | U | █ | R | O | U | N | D | █ | D | O | O | R |
| F | R | O | M | █ | S | U | L | K | Y | █ | E | T | U | I |
| A | L | P | S | █ | E | R | A | S | █ | █ | R | A | N | T |

**Solution:**

| D | A | D | A | | | S | E | M | I | | A | B | B | A |
|---|---|---|---|---|---|---|---|---|---|---|---|---|---|---|
| I | R | I | S | | S | C | R | U | B | | S | A | A | R |
| S | E | E | P | | P | R | I | D | E | | E | L | L | E |
| C | A | D | I | L | L | A | C | | R | A | P | I | D | S |
| | R | E | A | P | | A | I | N | T | | | | | |
| E | M | B | E | D | S | | O | V | A | T | I | O | N | |
| R | E | A | D | | H | O | P | O | N | | C | R | I | B |
| R | A | Y | | X | I | I | | | | A | G | O | | |
| S | T | O | P | | B | I | N | D | S | | S | T | E | W |
| | S | U | I | C | I | D | E | | P | E | T | E | R | S |
| | E | D | G | E | | N | O | V | A | | | | | |
| P | R | O | N | T | O | | B | A | K | E | R | I | E | S |
| O | A | H | U | | T | R | A | D | E | | R | O | D | E |
| S | N | I | T | | R | O | B | I | N | | E | W | E | R |
| E | G | O | S | | Y | E | A | R | | | D | A | N | E |

**Solution:**

| C | H | I | C |   |   | R | A | S | P |   | G | R | A | M |
| H | E | T | H |   | S | E | P | I | A |   | R | O | B | E |
| A | R | E | A |   | O | V | E | N | S |   | A | L | E | S |
| P | O | M | M | E | L | E | D |   | T | O | Y | O | T | A |
|   |   | O | P | A | L |   | G | O | N | E |   |   |   |   |
| Z | O | D | I | A | C |   | A | R | R | E | S | T | S |   |
| E | M | U | S |   | E | L | V | I | S |   | T | R | I | G |
| B | I | C |   |   | I | O | N |   |   |   | A | D | O |   |
| U | T | A | H |   | A | M | I | S | S |   | O | S | L | O |
|   | S | T | A | P | L | E | D |   | W | I | S | H | E | D |
|   |   | T | R | A | Y |   | B | E | N | T |   |   |   |   |
| F | A | B | L | E | S |   | A | L | A | C | R | I | T | Y |
| A | L | O | E |   | K | A | P | U | T |   | I | D | E | A |
| R | A | M | S |   | A | P | E | R | Y |   | C | L | A | W |
| O | R | B | S |   | N | E | X | T |   |   | H | Y | M | N |

**Solution:**

| S | P | A | S | | | O | A | R | S | | | A | L | M | A |
|---|---|---|---|---|---|---|---|---|---|---|---|---|---|---|---|
| W | A | S | P | | | I | N | J | U | N | | N | O | E | L |
| A | P | S | E | | | S | T | A | G | E | | T | O | N | E |
| T | A | N | C | O | L | O | R | | | A | N | I | M | U | S |
| | | | | T | R | A | P | | S | K | E | W | | | |
| C | A | R | E | E | N | | | A | C | E | T | A | T | E | |
| L | E | E | R | | | D | E | M | U | R | | R | O | L | L |
| E | S | C | | | | N | I | L | | | | W | E | E | |
| G | O | U | P | | | H | O | T | L | Y | | S | E | C | T |
| | | P | R | I | M | A | C | Y | | A | D | U | L | T | S |
| | | | A | R | C | H | | G | N | U | S | | | | |
| G | D | A | N | S | K | | C | A | K | E | P | A | N | S | |
| Y | O | G | I | | | L | E | A | V | E | | E | P | E | E |
| P | L | U | S | | | E | R | R | E | D | | C | I | T | E |
| S | L | A | T | | | Y | E | L | L | | | T | A | S | K |

**Solution:**

| P | R | E | P | | | B | E | A | U | | E | R | M | A |
| I | O | T | A | | P | R | A | N | K | | N | O | A | H |
| P | O | U | R | | S | A | T | Y | R | | L | O | C | O |
| S | K | I | L | L | E | T | S | | A | P | A | T | H | Y |
| | | | | O | P | U | S | | B | I | R | R | | |
| A | R | O | U | N | D | | S | E | N | E | G | A | L | |
| D | I | P | S | | O | C | H | R | E | | E | V | E | N |
| A | G | E | | | | A | I | R | | | | E | V | E |
| M | O | R | E | | A | R | R | A | S | | A | R | E | A |
| | R | A | T | A | B | L | E | | P | U | N | T | E | R |
| | | | C | I | A | O | | C | I | T | Y | | | |
| B | R | A | H | M | S | | N | I | C | E | T | I | E | S |
| L | E | V | I | | H | E | A | V | E | | I | D | E | A |
| A | D | E | N | | E | M | B | E | D | | M | O | L | L |
| B | O | R | G | | D | U | S | T | | | E | L | S | E |

**Solution:**

| P | E | R | U | ■ | ■ | O | B | I | E | ■ | C | O | L | D |
|---|---|---|---|---|---|---|---|---|---|---|---|---|---|---|
| O | R | E | S | ■ | B | L | O | O | M | ■ | R | O | A | R |
| N | I | N | E | ■ | A | D | D | U | P | ■ | E | Z | R | A |
| D | E | T | A | I | N | E | E | ■ | T | W | E | E | D | Y |
| ■ | ■ | ■ | C | O | N | N | ■ | P | I | E | D | ■ | ■ | ■ |
| A | R | C | A | N | E | ■ | D | I | E | T | A | R | Y | ■ |
| D | E | E | R | ■ | R | E | E | L | S | ■ | L | E | A | D |
| E | L | L | ■ | ■ | Q | U | O | ■ | ■ | F | R | I | ■ |
| N | I | L | E | ■ | D | U | C | T | S | ■ | P | E | N | N |
| ■ | C | O | T | E | R | I | E | ■ | C | O | U | R | S | E |
| ■ | ■ | H | E | A | P | ■ | N | A | P | E | ■ | ■ | ■ |
| D | E | V | I | L | S | ■ | P | A | N | T | R | I | E | S |
| E | P | I | C | ■ | T | O | A | S | T | ■ | I | D | E | A |
| B | E | T | A | ■ | I | N | L | A | Y | ■ | L | O | L | L |
| T | E | A | L | ■ | C | E | L | L | ■ | E | L | S | E |

**Solution:**

| N | A | S | A | | | L | U | N | G | | | C | A | M | P |
|---|---|---|---|---|---|---|---|---|---|---|---|---|---|---|---|
| O | P | A | L | | | S | A | T | Y | R | | E | V | I | L |
| A | S | I | A | | | T | R | A | C | E | | N | O | N | O |
| H | E | L | D | H | I | G | H | | N | I | T | W | I | T | |
| | | | | D | U | N | E | | O | D | O | R | | | |
| O | F | F | I | N | G | | O | P | E | N | E | R | S | | |
| B | E | E | N | | Y | O | D | E | L | | D | A | W | N | |
| O | A | R | | | P | I | N | | | | T | U | E | | |
| E | R | M | A | | R | E | U | S | E | | C | O | N | S | |
| | S | I | D | E | A | R | M | | C | L | I | N | G | S | |
| | | M | A | M | A | | C | H | O | P | | | | | |
| F | A | J | I | T | A | | F | O | O | T | H | O | L | D | |
| E | M | I | R | | D | R | I | V | E | | E | R | I | E | |
| T | I | M | E | | A | I | D | E | D | | R | A | M | P | |
| A | D | A | R | | N | O | E | S | | | S | L | O | T | |

**Solution:**

| B | A | R | B |   |   | L | O | C | O |   | O | P | A | L |
| O | R | E | O |   | C | L | A | S | P |   | A | L | M | A |
| S | E | A | M |   | A | O | R | T | A |   | R | U | M | P |
| C | A | D | B | U | R | Y | S |   | C | O | S | M | O | S |
|   |   |   | A | P | E | D |   | S | I | A | M |   |   |   |
| M | O | U | S | S | E |   | A | C | T | R | E | S | S |   |
| I | N | S | T |   | R | E | L | A | Y |   | N | A | T | O |
| S | S | E |   |   | N | I | L |   |   |   | I | O | N |   |
| S | E | R | E |   | R | E | B | E | L |   | S | L | I | T |
|   | T | S | U | N | A | M | I |   | U | N | E | S | C | O |
|   |   | T | O | N | Y |   | B | R | A | N |   |   |   |   |
| F | I | B | E | R | S |   | F | R | I | G | A | T | E | S |
| O | D | O | R |   | A | A | R | O | N |   | T | U | B | E |
| L | E | A | P |   | C | L | A | N | G |   | O | B | O | E |
| D | A | T | E |   | K | L | U | X |   |   | R | A | N | K |

**Solution:**

| H | A | S | P |  |  | F | U | G | I |  |  | B | E | R | G |
| O | R | E | O |  | V | E | N | O | M |  |  | A | W | O | L |
| S | E | A | T |  | E | V | I | T | A |  |  | Z | E | T | A |
| P | A | R | A | K | E | E | T |  | G | E | A | R | E | D |  |
|  |  |  | B | I | R | R |  | N | I | N | A |  |  |  |  |
| S | V | E | L | T | E |  | M | I | N | E | R | A | L |  |  |
| A | I | D | E |  | D | E | U | C | E |  | S | U | L | K |  |
| U | T | E |  |  |  | A | S | H |  |  |  | R | A | N |  |
| L | A | M | A |  | E | T | H | E | R |  | S | A | M | E |  |
|  | L | A | M | P | R | E | Y |  | O | U | T | L | A | W |  |
|  |  | M | O | R | N |  | L | O | S | E |  |  |  |  |  |
| P | E | L | O | T | A |  | D | E | M | E | R | S | A | L |  |
| O | M | A | N |  | N | E | R | V | E |  | I | N | C | A |  |
| K | I | W | I |  | D | R | U | I | D |  | L | A | R | K |  |
| E | T | N | A |  | S | E | B | S |  |  | E | P | E | E |  |

**Solution:**

| A | S | S | N |   |   | M | Y | T | H |   | W | A | S | P |
|---|---|---|---|---|---|---|---|---|---|---|---|---|---|---|
| F | A | L | A |   | G | O | O | E | Y |   | H | I | L | L |
| A | T | O | P |   | I | R | K | E | D |   | I | D | E | A |
| R | E | P | H | R | A | S | E |   | R | E | M | E | D | Y |
|   |   |   | T | O | N | E |   | O | A | R | S |   |   |   |
| C | A | C | H | E | T |   | G | U | N | N | E | R | S |   |
| O | K | R | A |   | S | C | O | T | T |   | Y | O | L | K |
| S | E | A |   | H | I | D |   |   |   |   | D | O | N |   |
| H | E | T | H |   | M | I | N | O | R |   | P | E | T | E |
|   | M | E | E | T | I | N | G |   | O | T | I | O | S | E |
|   |   | C | O | N | S |   | B | A | W | L |   |   |   |   |
| S | A | L | T | E | D |   | A | E | R | O | G | R | A | M |
| P | L | E | A |   | F | A | B | L | E |   | R | U | N | E |
| U | S | S | R |   | U | N | B | I | D |   | I | D | O | L |
| R | O | S | E |   | L | Y | R | E |   |   | M | E | N | D |

**Solution:**

| E | M | I | T | | | | B | E | A | M | | | S | H | E | D |
|---|---|---|---|---|---|---|---|---|---|---|---|---|---|---|---|---|
| B | O | S | H | | | S | A | M | B | A | | | T | E | A | R |
| B | A | L | I | | | P | L | U | S | H | | | E | A | S | Y |
| S | T | E | E | P | L | E | S | | | A | L | E | R | T | S | |
| | | | | V | O | I | D | | | A | T | O | P | | | |
| V | O | T | E | I | N | | | C | O | M | P | L | E | X | | |
| A | R | E | S | | | T | E | R | R | A | | | E | D | E | N |
| I | B | M | | | | | V | A | T | | | | U | N | O | |
| N | I | P | S | | | V | I | S | A | S | | | E | C | O | N |
| | | T | O | O | M | U | C | H | | | E | U | G | E | N | E |
| | | | | M | E | L | T | | | P | A | S | O | | | |
| A | C | C | E | N | T | | | H | A | M | S | T | E | R | S | |
| H | O | H | O | | | U | S | A | G | E | | | I | C | O | N |
| E | L | A | N | | | R | A | V | E | N | | | S | H | O | O |
| M | A | T | E | | | E | W | E | R | | | | T | O | M | B |

**Solution:**

| S | A | G | A | | | R | A | G | U | | C | H | U | M |
|---|---|---|---|---|---|---|---|---|---|---|---|---|---|---|
| P | E | O | N | | B | E | F | O | G | | H | I | R | E |
| I | R | A | N | | L | A | R | V | A | | A | S | S | N |
| C | O | L | O | R | A | D | O | | N | A | S | S | A | U |
| | | | Y | A | M | S | | A | D | D | S | | | |
| R | E | N | E | G | E | | F | R | A | M | I | N | G | |
| E | M | I | R | | S | A | L | O | N | | S | O | U | P |
| E | E | G | | | B | U | S | | | | | L | I | E |
| K | N | E | W | | P | L | I | E | D | | K | A | L | E |
| | D | R | I | L | L | E | D | | R | U | I | N | E | R |
| | | G | E | A | R | | S | O | F | T | | | | |
| O | R | E | G | O | N | | P | I | V | O | T | I | N | G |
| V | I | A | L | | E | T | U | D | E | | E | C | O | N |
| A | P | S | E | | T | E | L | L | S | | N | O | V | A |
| L | E | E | S | | S | A | L | E | | | S | N | O | W |

**Solution:**

| A | B | B | A | ■ | ■ | C | L | E | G | ■ | N | E | S | T |
|---|---|---|---|---|---|---|---|---|---|---|---|---|---|---|
| M | O | O | N | ■ | C | H | O | S | E | ■ | A | C | H | E |
| O | S | L | O | ■ | R | U | S | T | Y | ■ | B | O | O | S |
| S | H | O | T | G | U | N | S | ■ | S | P | I | N | E | T |
| ■ | ■ | ■ | H | U | S | K | ■ | P | E | T | S | ■ | ■ | ■ |
| A | C | C | E | N | T | ■ | M | I | R | A | C | L | E | ■ |
| S | L | U | R | ■ | S | N | I | P | S | ■ | O | U | T | S |
| E | A | R | ■ | ■ | ■ | E | N | E | ■ | ■ | ■ | C | U | E |
| A | S | I | A | ■ | I | V | O | R | Y | ■ | T | I | D | E |
| ■ | P | A | R | T | N | E | R | ■ | O | X | I | D | E | S |
| ■ | ■ | ■ | D | E | E | R | ■ | S | U | I | T | ■ | ■ | ■ |
| V | A | L | U | E | R | ■ | S | A | T | I | A | B | L | E |
| O | R | E | O | ■ | T | H | I | G | H | ■ | N | A | I | L |
| L | I | E | U | ■ | I | O | T | A | S | ■ | I | L | L | S |
| T | A | R | S | ■ | A | G | E | S | ■ | ■ | C | I | T | E |

**Solution:**

| O | G | L | E | ■ | ■ | S | A | G | E | ■ | C | U | F | F |
| W | R | E | N | ■ | U | N | B | O | X | ■ | O | S | L | O |
| N | O | V | A | ■ | S | A | U | D | I | ■ | A | E | O | N |
| S | W | I | M | S | U | I | T | ■ | G | I | R | D | E | D |
| ■ | ■ | ■ | E | A | R | L | ■ | M | E | N | S | ■ | ■ | ■ |
| S | V | E | L | T | E | ■ | T | I | N | K | E | R | S | ■ |
| E | E | L | S | ■ | R | A | B | A | T | ■ | R | O | U | T |
| A | X | E | ■ | ■ | ■ | T | O | M | ■ | ■ | ■ | A | S | H |
| T | E | C | H | ■ | M | I | N | I | M | ■ | A | C | H | E |
| ■ | S | T | E | R | I | L | E | ■ | U | R | C | H | I | N |
| ■ | ■ | ■ | C | O | L | T | ■ | S | T | Y | E | ■ | ■ | ■ |
| R | I | S | K | E | D | ■ | P | H | A | E | T | O | N | S |
| A | B | E | L | ■ | E | C | L | A | T | ■ | A | R | E | A |
| G | I | B | E | ■ | S | W | O | R | E | ■ | T | A | S | K |
| U | S | S | R | ■ | T | A | P | E | ■ | ■ | E | L | S | E |

**Solution:**

| O | G | L | E |   |   |   | S | A | G | E |   | C | U | F | F |
| W | R | E | N |   |   | U | N | B | O | X |   | O | S | L | O |
| N | O | V | A |   |   | S | A | U | D | I |   | A | E | O | N |
| S | W | I | M | S | U | I | T |   | G | I | R | D | E | D |   |
|   |   |   |   | E | A | R | L |   | M | E | N | S |   |   |   |
| S | V | E | L | T | E |   | T | I | N | K | E | R | S |   |   |
| E | E | L | S |   | R | A | B | A | T |   | R | O | U | T |   |
| A | X | E |   |   |   | T | O | M |   |   |   | A | S | H |   |
| T | E | C | H |   | M | I | N | I | M |   | A | C | H | E |   |
|   | S | T | E | R | I | L | E |   | U | R | C | H | I | N |   |
|   |   | C | O | L | T |   | S | T | Y | E |   |   |   |   |   |
| R | I | S | K | E | D |   | P | H | A | E | T | O | N | S |   |
| A | B | E | L |   | E | C | L | A | T |   | A | R | E | A |   |
| G | I | B | E |   | S | W | O | R | E |   | T | A | S | K |   |
| U | S | S | R |   | T | A | P | E |   |   | E | L | S | E |   |

**Solution:**

| G | R | A | F |  |  | S | A | W | S |  |  | P | A | D | S |
|---|---|---|---|---|---|---|---|---|---|---|---|---|---|---|---|
| L | I | M | O |  | A | L | I | B | I |  |  | A | L | O | E |
| O | V | E | R |  | M | A | N | N | A |  |  | C | U | T | E |
| B | E | N | E | D | I | C | T |  |  | M | A | I | M | E | D |
|  |  |  |  | R | I | C | K |  | S | E | R | F |  |  |  |
| T | E | L | U | G | U |  | T | A | S | T | I | N | G |  |  |
| Z | I | O | N |  | S | A | U | T | E |  | C | U | R | B |  |
| A | D | O |  |  |  | B | R | A |  |  |  |  | L | E | O |
| R | E | S | T |  | H | E | N | N | A |  | F | L | A | N |  |
|  | R | E | V | E | A | L | S |  | C | H | A | S | T | E |  |
|  |  |  | R | A | R | E |  | S | T | U | N |  |  |  |  |
| A | D | S | O | R | B |  | B | O | U | N | C | I | N | G |  |
| S | I | L | O |  | O | P | E | R | A |  |  | I | D | O | L |
| S | K | I | M |  | R | E | V | E | L |  |  | E | L | S | E |
| N | E | T | S |  | S | A | Y | S |  |  |  | S | E | E | N |

**Solution:**

| C | L | E | F |   |   | S | Y | L | I |   |   | S | Y | N | C |
| Z | E | A | L |   | S | E | W | E | D |   | H | A | I | L |   |
| A | N | T | E |   | M | C | C | O | Y |   | I | N | C | A |   |
| R | O | S | A | R | I | T | A |   | L | O | N | G | E | D |   |
|   |   |   | B | A | R | S |   | G | L | A | D |   |   |   |   |
| S | Q | U | A | W | K |   | U | N | I | T | I | N | G |   |   |
| H | U | N | G |   | S | U | M | A | C |   | G | Y | R | O |   |
| O | A | F |   |   | S | B | W |   |   | L | A | W |   |   |   |
| E | D | I | T |   | G | U | E | S | T |   | C | O | D | E |   |
|   | S | T | E | L | L | A | R |   | I | R | O | N | E | D |   |
|   |   | R | O | I | L |   | D | R | E | W |   |   |   |   |   |
| P | O | G | R | O | M |   | L | O | A | D | A | B | L | E |   |
| T | H | A | I |   | P | R | A | W | N |   | R | A | I | L |   |
| S | I | G | N |   | S | A | U | N | A |   | D | I | E | S |   |
| D | O | S | E |   | E | D | D | Y |   |   | S | L | U | E |   |

**Solution:**

| F | I | B | S | | | | A | C | E | S | | | B | A | W | L |
| I | D | L | E | | | S | P | L | A | T | | | A | R | E | A |
| S | E | E | N | | | C | H | U | T | E | | | B | I | A | S |
| C | A | U | S | E | R | I | E | | R | O | Y | A | L | S | | |
| | | | | | A | G | E | D | | E | N | D | S | | | |
| B | E | S | T | O | W | | W | E | L | D | I | N | G | | | |
| A | X | L | E | | S | T | O | R | Y | | T | I | R | E | | |
| C | P | A | | | | O | U | I | | | | H | A | Y | | |
| H | O | N | E | | A | P | N | E | A | | C | I | T | E | | |
| | S | T | U | B | B | E | D | | F | O | U | L | E | D | | |
| | | P | O | U | R | | T | R | A | P | | | | | | |
| U | P | S | H | O | T | | D | I | E | T | C | O | K | E | | |
| S | O | L | O | | T | W | I | N | S | | A | X | I | S | | |
| E | L | A | N | | E | A | R | T | H | | K | E | E | P | | |
| D | O | P | Y | | D | Y | E | S | | | E | N | V | Y | | |

**Solution:**

| A | B | B | A |   |   |   | T | W | O | S |   | A | C | T | S |
| R | E | A | L |   |   | S | Y | R | I | A |   | R | O | I | L |
| C | A | L | M |   |   | P | S | A | L | M |   | M | O | D | E |
| H | U | L | A | H | O | O | P |   | O | R | A | T | E | D |   |
|   |   |   |   | N | E | O | N |   | A | V | I | D |   |   |   |
| N | E | W | A | R | K |   | M | B | A | B | A | N | E |   |   |
| E | R | I | C |   | S | C | O | U | R |   | S | A | Y | S |   |
| B | U | D |   |   |   | H | A | S |   |   |   | K | I | A |   |
| E | P | E | E |   | W | I | N | E | S |   | B | E | N | T |   |
|   | T | R | A | C | E | R | S |   | P | L | E | D | G | E |   |
|   |   |   | S | W | A | P |   | R | I | O | T |   |   |   |   |
| O | P | T | I | O | N |   | R | I | G | O | R | O | U | S |   |
| R | A | R | E |   |   | I | M | A | G | O |   | A | L | S | O |
| E | G | I | S |   |   | N | I | G | H | T |   | Y | E | A | R |
| S | E | P | T |   |   | G | L | U | T |   |   | S | O | F | T |

**Solution:**

| C | A | I | N | | | | S | E | B | S | | | E | T | N | A |
|---|---|---|---|---|---|---|---|---|---|---|---|---|---|---|---|---|
| O | N | C | E | | | S | P | L | I | T | | | M | E | O | W |
| S | T | O | W | | | C | I | S | C | O | | | P | A | P | A |
| T | I | N | Y | T | R | E | E | | | N | I | A | M | E | Y | |
| | | | | O | W | E | D | | | L | I | N | T | | | |
| E | S | C | R | O | W | | | M | U | N | C | H | E | S | | |
| L | O | O | K | | | S | T | A | G | G | | | Y | A | N | G |
| L | A | B | | | | | I | C | E | | | | | T | O | O |
| E | R | R | S | | | J | E | R | R | Y | | | A | E | R | O |
| | S | A | P | P | O | R | O | | | E | A | R | N | E | D | |
| | | | R | I | B | S | | | P | A | R | T | | | | |
| S | A | M | U | E | L | | | H | U | S | K | I | E | S | T | |
| O | P | E | C | | | E | X | A | L | T | | | S | T | Y | E |
| I | S | L | E | | | S | I | S | S | Y | | | T | U | N | A |
| L | E | T | S | | | S | I | T | E | | | | S | I | C | K |

**Solution:**

| D | U | P | E |   |   | H | I | F | I |   | B | A | U | D |
|---|---|---|---|---|---|---|---|---|---|---|---|---|---|---|
| A | S | E | A |   | Z | E | B | E | C |   | A | L | S | O |
| D | E | E | R |   | O | X | I | D | E |   | L | I | S | P |
| O | R | P | H | A | N | E | D |   | B | E | L | F | R | Y |
|   |   | A | X | I | S |   | A | U | T | O |   |   |   |   |
| B | A | R | R | E | N |   | S | C | R | A | T | C | H |   |
| O | M | I | T |   | G | O | I | N | G |   | S | A | I | D |
| S | O | N |   |   | I | R | E |   |   |   | N | N | E |   |
| C | U | S | P |   | S | L | E | D | S |   | S | A | G | E |
|   | R | E | S | U | M | E | S |   | L | U | L | L | E | D |
|   |   | A | F | A | R |   | M | E | T | E |   |   |   |   |
| H | E | L | L | O | S |   | W | I | D | E | N | I | N | G |
| E | M | I | T |   | H | Y | I | N | G |   | D | O | O | R |
| F | U | M | E |   | E | E | R | I | E |   | E | T | U | I |
| T | S | A | R |   | S | T | E | M |   |   | R | A | N | T |

**Solution:**

| B | A | C | H | | | P | O | M | P | | | C | A | F | E |
|---|---|---|---|---|---|---|---|---|---|---|---|---|---|---|---|
| A | G | U | A | | | P | L | A | T | O | | | O | V | E | N |
| T | U | R | N | | | L | A | R | V | A | | | L | O | R | D |
| H | E | E | D | L | E | S | S | | | C | L | O | W | N | S |
| | | | | S | P | A | M | | | W | H | Y | S | | |
| A | D | D | E | N | D | | | C | H | E | E | S | E | S | |
| R | O | U | T | | | S | O | L | A | R | | | I | N | T | O |
| T | I | C | | | | | D | O | C | | | | | S | E | A |
| S | N | A | P | | | V | O | D | K | A | | | S | U | I | T |
| | G | L | I | D | E | R | S | | | G | R | E | E | N | S |
| | | | C | O | N | S | | | G | R | A | M | | | |
| M | O | R | A | L | E | | | E | R | E | M | I | T | I | C |
| A | R | E | S | | | E | E | R | I | E | | | N | U | D | E |
| L | E | N | S | | | R | E | I | N | S | | | A | B | E | L |
| T | O | T | O | | | S | L | E | D | | | | R | E | A | L |

**Solution:**

| D | U | P | E |   |   | H | I | F | I |   | B | A | U | D |
| A | S | E | A |   | Z | E | B | E | C |   | A | L | S | O |
| D | E | E | R |   | O | X | I | D | E |   | L | I | S | P |
| O | R | P | H | A | N | E | D |   | B | E | L | F | R | Y |
|   |   |   | A | X | I | S |   | A | U | T | O |   |   |   |
| B | A | R | R | E | N |   | S | C | R | A | T | C | H |   |
| O | M | I | T |   | G | O | I | N | G |   | S | A | I | D |
| S | O | N |   |   | I | R | E |   |   |   | N | N | E |
| C | U | S | P |   | S | L | E | D | S |   | S | A | G | E |
|   | R | E | S | U | M | E | S |   | L | U | L | L | E | D |
|   |   |   | A | F | A | R |   | M | E | T | E |   |   |   |
| H | E | L | L | O | S |   | W | I | D | E | N | I | N | G |
| E | M | I | T |   | H | Y | I | N | G |   | D | O | O | R |
| F | U | M | E |   | E | E | R | I | E |   | E | T | U | I |
| T | S | A | R |   | S | T | E | M |   |   | R | A | N | T |

**Solution:**

| B | A | C | H | | | P | O | M | P | | | C | A | F | E |
|---|---|---|---|---|---|---|---|---|---|---|---|---|---|---|---|
| A | G | U | A | | P | L | A | T | O | | | O | V | E | N |
| T | U | R | N | | L | A | R | V | A | | | L | O | R | D |
| H | E | E | D | L | E | S | S | | C | L | O | W | N | S | |
| | | | | S | P | A | M | | W | H | Y | S | | | |
| A | D | D | E | N | D | | C | H | E | E | S | E | S | | |
| R | O | U | T | | S | O | L | A | R | | I | N | T | O | |
| T | I | C | | | D | O | C | | | | S | E | A | | |
| S | N | A | P | | V | O | D | K | A | | S | U | I | T | |
| | G | L | I | D | E | R | S | | G | R | E | E | N | S | |
| | | C | O | N | S | | G | R | A | M | | | | | |
| M | O | R | A | L | E | | E | R | E | M | I | T | I | C | |
| A | R | E | S | | E | E | R | I | E | | N | U | D | E | |
| L | E | N | S | | R | E | I | N | S | | A | B | E | L | |
| T | O | T | O | | S | L | E | D | | | R | E | A | L | |

**Solution:**

| P | L | E | A | | | | T | O | T | O | | E | M | U | S |
|---|---|---|---|---|---|---|---|---|---|---|---|---|---|---|---|
| R | A | P | T | | | C | H | I | E | F | | N | O | S | E |
| O | M | I | T | | | R | E | N | E | W | | G | L | E | N |
| F | A | C | E | M | A | S | K | | R | A | R | E | S | T | |
| | | | | M | A | N | E | | G | A | L | A | | | |
| S | A | M | P | L | E | | D | U | T | I | F | U | L | | |
| P | L | A | T | | S | L | O | S | H | | T | S | A | R | |
| I | B | M | | | | Y | E | T | | | | A | G | E | |
| C | U | B | E | | E | N | R | O | L | | E | G | O | S | |
| | M | A | N | I | A | C | S | | I | N | G | E | S | T | |
| | | G | O | S | H | | | S | L | O | G | | | | |
| B | E | I | R | U | T | | S | T | A | N | D | O | U | T | |
| A | L | S | O | | | E | T | H | I | C | | I | N | T | O |
| I | L | L | S | | | R | O | I | L | S | | S | T | A | G |
| L | E | E | S | | | N | O | P | E | | | H | O | H | O |

**Solution:**

| A | C | A | D |   |   | R | A | G | U |   | A | P | S | E |
|---|---|---|---|---|---|---|---|---|---|---|---|---|---|---|
| T | H | E | E |   | M | A | D | A | M |   | P | R | O | S |
| O | A | R | S |   | O | R | A | L | B |   | H | E | L | P |
| P | R | O | P | O | S | E | R |   | R | E | A | S | O | N |
|   |   |   | A | F | A | R |   | B | A | G | S |   |   |   |
| T | A | H | I | T | I |   | B | E | G | G | I | N | G |   |
| A | L | A | R |   | C | L | O | S | E |   | C | O | R | D |
| I | I | I |   |   |   | I | W | O |   |   |   | V | I | A |
| L | A | R | D |   | U | N | I | T | S |   | S | A | L | T |
|   | S | Y | R | I | N | G | E |   | T | O | U | S | L | E |
|   |   | U | N | D | O |   | B | R | A | D |   |   |   |   |
| W | H | E | N | C | E |   | H | U | A | R | A | C | H | E |
| R | A | C | K |   | R | E | E | D | Y |   | F | O | A | L |
| A | L | O | E |   | G | O | A | D | S |   | E | R | R | S |
| P | E | N | N |   | O | N | L | Y |   |   | D | E | M | E |

**Solution:**

| H | A | N | D | ■ | ■ | L | A | V | A | ■ | R | O | B | E |
|---|---|---|---|---|---|---|---|---|---|---|---|---|---|---|
| U | S | E | R | ■ | T | E | L | E | X | ■ | E | P | E | E |
| S | E | B | E | ■ | H | A | I | T | I | ■ | T | E | A | L |
| H | A | N | D | S | O | F | F | ■ | A | M | I | C | U | S |
| ■ | ■ | G | A | M | Y | ■ | K | L | A | N | ■ | ■ | ■ | ■ |
| S | E | N | E | C | A | ■ | B | O | L | L | A | R | D | ■ |
| I | R | I | S | ■ | S | T | R | A | Y | ■ | L | I | R | A |
| A | R | E | ■ | ■ | H | A | L | ■ | ■ | ■ | V | I | P | ■ |
| M | O | C | K | ■ | S | I | N | A | I | ■ | P | A | V | E |
| ■ | R | E | N | A | M | E | D | ■ | N | A | I | L | E | D |
| ■ | ■ | U | S | A | F | ■ | F | U | L | L | ■ | ■ | ■ | ■ |
| E | P | O | C | H | S | ■ | R | A | R | I | F | I | E | D |
| T | A | S | K | ■ | H | E | A | V | E | ■ | E | D | D | Y |
| N | U | L | L | ■ | E | G | G | O | S | ■ | R | E | E | K |
| A | L | O | E | ■ | D | O | U | R | ■ | ■ | S | A | N | E |

**Solution:**

| C | R | I | B |   |   |   | A | M | E | N |   | B | O | T | A |
|---|---|---|---|---|---|---|---|---|---|---|---|---|---|---|---|
| H | A | L | O |   |   | S | P | A | R | E |   | A | B | E | L |
| U | G | L | Y |   |   | U | S | U | R | P |   | R | O | L | L |
| M | U | S | C | A | T | E | L |   | H | U | G | E | L | Y |   |
|   |   |   |   | O | P | U | S |   | M | E | S | A |   |   |   |
| E | M | O | T | E | R |   | B | E | W | A | I | L | S |   |   |
| G | E | N | T |   | E | X | I | T | S |   | N | E | A | T |   |
| G | A | S |   |   |   | E | N | E |   |   |   | A | B | R |   |
| S | L | E | D |   | A | N | D | R | E |   | A | F | R | O |   |
|   | S | T | U | D | I | O | S |   | P | R | E | Y | E | D |   |
|   |   | K | I | L | N |   | D | O | O | R |   |   |   |   |   |
| S | L | E | E | V | E |   | S | E | C | T | I | O | N | S |   |
| W | A | R | D |   | R | A | L | P | H |   | A | B | U | T |   |
| A | M | M | O |   | O | R | E | O | S |   | L | I | K | E |   |
| T | E | A | M |   | N | E | W | T |   |   | S | E | E | P |   |

**Solution:**

| B | A | R | B | ■ | ■ | P | O | S | E | ■ | M | I | C | A |
|---|---|---|---|---|---|---|---|---|---|---|---|---|---|---|
| A | G | A | R | ■ | S | H | I | R | R | ■ | I | C | O | N |
| N | O | N | O | ■ | M | A | N | I | A | ■ | L | E | N | O |
| E | G | G | W | H | I | S | K | ■ | S | O | D | D | E | N |
| ■ | ■ | ■ | N | O | T | E | ■ | S | E | B | E | ■ | ■ | ■ |
| S | L | E | I | G | H | ■ | P | U | R | I | S | T | S | ■ |
| W | I | N | E | ■ | Y | A | R | D | S | ■ | T | R | I | P |
| A | B | R | ■ | ■ | ■ | S | O | S | ■ | ■ | ■ | E | N | E |
| P | R | O | S | ■ | L | I | B | Y | A | ■ | L | A | C | E |
| ■ | A | L | C | A | I | D | E | ■ | L | O | I | T | E | R |
| ■ | ■ | H | Y | P | E | ■ | E | L | A | N | ■ | ■ | ■ | ■ |
| V | E | N | E | E | R | ■ | S | M | I | R | K | I | N | G |
| I | T | E | M | ■ | E | D | U | C | E | ■ | A | B | E | L |
| S | U | R | E | ■ | A | R | C | E | D | ■ | G | I | B | E |
| A | I | D | S | ■ | D | Y | K | E | ■ | ■ | E | D | E | N |

**Solution:**

| A | C | A | D |   |   | I | B | I | S |   | B | R | A | T |
|---|---|---|---|---|---|---|---|---|---|---|---|---|---|---|
| R | O | L | O |   | S | C | A | L | P |   | E | A | C | H |
| M | O | O | N |   | K | I | L | L | A |   | A | R | E | A |
| S | T | E | A | D | I | E | D |   | R | A | R | E | S | T |
|   |   |   | H | E | R | R |   | K | I | T | E |   |   |   |
| F | L | A | U | N | T |   | U | N | N | E | R | V | E |   |
| L | O | N | E |   | S | H | R | U | G |   | S | A | S | S |
| E | G | G |   |   |   | A | B | R |   |   |   | U | T | E |
| W | I | L | E |   | O | R | A | L | B |   | G | L | E | N |
|   | C | O | N | T | E | M | N |   | E | D | I | T | E | D |
|   |   | D | U | D | S |   | S | W | A | N |   |   |   |   |
| I | N | C | U | B | I |   | S | P | A | N | G | L | E | D |
| R | O | A | R |   | P | E | T | E | R |   | H | A | Z | Y |
| A | N | N | E |   | A | P | A | C | E |   | A | C | R | E |
| N | E | E | D |   | L | A | Y | S |   |   | M | E | A | D |

**Solution:**

| P | A | T | H | | | M | A | L | E | | N | E | A | T |
|---|---|---|---|---|---|---|---|---|---|---|---|---|---|---|
| U | R | S | A | | T | E | L | E | X | | I | D | L | E |
| P | E | A | R | | H | A | I | T | I | | C | A | S | E |
| A | A | R | D | W | O | L | F | | G | N | O | M | O | N |
| | | | T | O | R | Y | | K | E | Y | S | | | |
| U | P | T | O | W | N | | F | A | N | C | I | E | R | |
| S | E | E | P | | S | H | O | R | T | | A | X | E | D |
| S | S | E | | | | E | R | A | | | | A | G | O |
| R | O | T | C | | F | I | A | T | S | | E | L | A | N |
| | S | H | O | W | E | R | Y | | M | A | N | T | L | E |
| | | M | O | S | S | | L | E | G | S | | | | |
| U | P | R | O | O | T | | S | I | L | E | N | C | E | R |
| P | O | O | R | | O | C | T | E | T | | A | L | P | O |
| O | N | T | O | | O | P | E | N | S | | R | U | E | D |
| N | E | S | S | | N | A | P | S | | | L | E | E | S |

**Solution:**

| A | F | E | W |   |   | O | G | R | E |   | H | O | E | S |
|---|---|---|---|---|---|---|---|---|---|---|---|---|---|---|
| B | A | R | E |   | A | B | O | U | T |   | E | U | R | O |
| B | R | I | E |   | Z | E | B | E | C |   | A | S | I | A |
| R | O | C | K | M | O | S | S |   | H | A | L | T | E | R |
|   |   |   | D | A | R | E |   | L | I | N | T |   |   |   |
| R | O | T | A | T | E |   | T | I | N | Y | H | A | T |   |
| A | W | A | Y |   | S | L | I | N | G |   | Y | E | A | R |
| N | I | P |   |   |   | L | A | G |   |   |   | S | B | E |
| K | N | E | W |   | A | A | R | O | N |   | N | O | O | N |
|   | G | R | A | N | D | M | A |   | I | S | O | P | O | D |
|   |   |   | D | I | V | A |   | S | P | O | T |   |   |   |
| M | E | D | D | L | E |   | P | E | P | T | I | D | I | C |
| O | P | A | L |   | R | E | E | V | E |   | C | O | D | A |
| S | E | R | E |   | B | A | R | E | D |   | E | V | E | R |
| T | E | N | D |   | S | T | U | N |   |   | D | E | A | D |

**Solution:**

| S | H | U | T |   |   |   | O | K | R | A |   |   | E | R | M | A |
| N | O | S | E |   |   | U | S | E | U | P |   |   | M | A | I | D |
| A | S | S | N |   |   | S | C | E | N | E |   |   | I | N | C | H |
| P | E | R | S | O | N | A | L |   |   | L | O | N | G | E | D |   |
|   |   |   |   | E | W | E | R |   | J | I | B | E |   |   |   |   |
| C | U | R | L | E | W |   | B | I | K | I | N | I | S |   |   |   |
| A | S | H | Y |   | S | H | A | M | E |   | T | S | A | R |   |   |
| B | U | Y |   |   |   | E | L | M |   |   |   | L | I | E |   |   |
| S | A | M | E |   | A | L | K | Y | D | M | A | L | L |   |   |   |
|   | L | E | G | A | L | L | Y |   | W | H | I | M | S | Y |   |   |
|   |   | O | N | T | O |   | D | E | A | N |   |   |   |   |   |   |
| P | L | A | T | T | E |   | O | I | L | S | T | O | N | E |   |   |
| T | I | K | I |   | R | E | B | E | L |   | A | P | I | A |   |   |
| A | V | I | S |   | E | M | I | T | S |   | G | A | B | S |   |   |
| S | E | N | T |   | D | U | E | S |   |   | E | L | S | E |   |   |

**Solution:**

| B | A | S | K |   |   | B | E | T | A |   | N | A | S | A |
| E | C | O | N |   | L | I | L | A | C |   | I | B | I | S |
| T | H | A | I |   | A | G | A | P | E |   | E | E | L | S |
| H | E | P | T | A | G | O | N |   | T | E | L | L | O | N |
|   |   |   | T | R | O | T |   | O | I | L | S |   |   |   |
| H | A | V | E | T | O |   | S | U | F | F | E | R | S |   |
| A | V | I | D |   | N | I | T | T | Y |   | N | A | P | S |
| R | O | D |   |   |   | R | I | G |   |   |   | D | U | O |
| E | W | E | R |   | D | O | N | O | R |   | B | I | R | R |
|   | S | O | I | L | I | N | G |   | O | B | O | I | S | T |
|   |   | P | I | T | Y |   | A | B | U | T |   |   |   |   |
| J | O | S | E | P | H |   | C | R | E | S | T | I | N | G |
| U | P | O | N |   | E | R | R | O | R |   | O | D | O | R |
| G | A | M | E |   | R | O | A | S | T |   | M | O | V | E |
| S | L | E | D |   | S | E | B | E |   |   | S | L | A | Y |

**Solution:**

| B | A | T | H | | | S | O | U | P | | D | E | B | T |
|---|---|---|---|---|---|---|---|---|---|---|---|---|---|---|
| L | U | R | E | | T | E | M | P | O | | E | P | E | E |
| O | R | A | L | | W | R | E | S | T | | L | I | M | A |
| C | A | M | P | A | I | G | N | | L | A | I | C | A | L |
| | | | O | G | R | E | | B | U | R | G | | | |
| R | E | F | U | E | L | | B | A | C | K | H | O | E | |
| O | M | I | T | | S | P | E | C | K | | T | A | X | I |
| B | O | O | | | A | G | O | | | | S | A | D | |
| E | T | N | A | | S | E | I | N | E | | H | I | L | L |
| | E | A | S | T | M | A | N | | Y | E | A | S | T | Y |
| | P | E | O | N | | J | E | S | S | | | | | |
| R | E | V | E | A | L | | C | O | L | E | S | L | A | W |
| E | R | I | C | | D | E | L | H | I | | L | I | M | O |
| D | I | N | T | | E | M | E | N | D | | E | V | E | N |
| S | E | E | S | | R | U | G | S | | | | D | E | N | T |

**Solution:**

| B | A | T | H | | | S | A | R | I | | K | E | E | L |
|---|---|---|---|---|---|---|---|---|---|---|---|---|---|---|
| A | S | I | A | | S | H | R | U | G | | N | U | D | E |
| S | E | E | R | | W | O | M | E | N | | I | R | I | S |
| H | A | R | D | C | O | P | Y | | I | N | G | O | T | S |
| | | | | T | W | O | S | | U | T | A | H | | |
| T | Y | C | O | O | N | | I | N | E | P | T | L | Y | |
| R | E | A | P | | S | A | L | A | D | | S | O | O | T |
| O | A | R | | | | F | I | R | | | | B | U | Y |
| D | R | A | B | | S | T | A | Y | S | | H | A | R | P |
| | S | T | O | M | P | E | D | | H | O | A | R | S | E |
| | | | B | U | R | R | | J | A | B | S | | | |
| P | L | A | S | M | A | | J | U | R | I | S | T | I | C |
| L | U | L | L | | W | O | U | L | D | | L | I | R | A |
| O | B | O | E | | L | A | N | E | S | | E | R | A | S |
| D | E | E | D | | S | T | O | P | | | D | E | N | T |

**Solution:**

| F | A | T | E |  |  | A | M | I | D |  | A | H | O | Y |
|---|---|---|---|---|---|---|---|---|---|---|---|---|---|---|
| I | R | A | N |  | B | A | Y | O | U |  | N | O | V | A |
| S | I | L | T |  | A | N | N | U | L |  | O | P | E | N |
| H | A | C | I | E | N | D | A |  | L | A | D | I | N | G |
|  |  |  | C | L | A | W |  | O | I | L | Y |  |  |  |
| S | O | L | E | M | N |  | A | W | N | I | N | G | S |  |
| P | A | L | S |  | A | W | I | N | G |  | E | A | T | S |
| A | K | A |  |  | O | D | E |  |  | M | I | L |
| M | E | M | O | E | V | E | R | Y |  | V | I | L | A |
|  | N | A | T | I | V | E | S |  | O | P | E | N | L | Y |
|  | T | W | I | N |  | E | R | R | S |  |  |  |
| S | C | H | O | O | L |  | M | A | K | E | S | M | A | D |
| L | O | O | M |  | E | R | A | S | E |  | E | A | S | E |
| U | R | S | A |  | S | A | Y | E | R |  | L | I | E | N |
| E | D | E | N |  | T | W | O | S |  | S | L | A | T |

**Solution:**

```
F E A R ■ ■ U S D A ■ E D G Y
L A N E ■ A N T I C ■ S O L O
A C T S ■ S C O T T ■ T R I G
W H I T E C A P ■ R H O M B I
■ ■ ■ S T E P ■ V E I N ■ ■
O H I O A N ■ S I S T I N E ■
M O R N ■ D E M O S ■ A I D T
E P A ■ ■ V O L ■ ■ E G O
N E T S ■ R E C A P ■ A C E S
■ R E T H I N K ■ O F F E R S
■ ■ R I O T ■ C L U E ■ ■
D R E A M T ■ G H A N A I A N
R U B Y ■ O N I O N ■ R O B E
A L O E ■ U N B I D ■ E W E R
B E N D ■ S E E R ■ ■ D A D O
```

**Solution:**

| S | L | U | G | | | C | H | A | D | | S | P | I | C |
|---|---|---|---|---|---|---|---|---|---|---|---|---|---|---|
| N | A | S | A | | D | O | Y | L | E | | H | I | R | E |
| A | V | E | R | | R | A | D | I | X | | E | C | O | N |
| G | A | R | G | O | Y | L | E | | T | Y | R | A | N | T |
| | | | | L | A | O | S | | C | R | I | B | | |
| M | A | S | E | R | U | | S | H | A | P | E | L | Y | |
| A | L | P | S | | T | O | W | E | L | | T | O | E | D |
| C | I | A | | | R | E | F | | | | | N | N | E |
| H | A | R | M | | F | A | L | S | E | | J | E | T | S |
| | S | E | A | W | A | L | L | | A | N | O | R | A | K |
| | | C | H | U | B | | E | T | U | I | | | | |
| D | A | R | R | Y | L | | E | V | E | N | N | E | S | S |
| A | R | E | A | | T | A | P | I | R | | T | R | O | T |
| S | I | A | M | | E | X | I | T | S | | L | I | M | A |
| H | A | R | E | | D | E | C | A | | | Y | E | A | R |

**Solution:**

| A | D | A | R | | | A | G | U | A | | S | M | U | G |
|---|---|---|---|---|---|---|---|---|---|---|---|---|---|---|
| M | E | M | O | | S | T | U | N | G | | Y | O | R | E |
| O | L | E | O | | H | A | N | O | I | | S | A | G | A |
| K | I | N | S | F | O | L | K | | L | E | T | T | E | R |
| | | | | T | R | U | E | | T | I | M | E | | |
| A | B | S | E | I | L | | B | I | T | U | M | E | N | |
| P | E | E | R | | D | O | I | L | Y | | S | L | U | E |
| E | R | R | | | W | A | D | | | | | F | R | Y |
| D | E | E | R | | I | N | L | E | T | | R | I | S | E |
| | T | R | O | L | L | E | Y | | A | T | O | N | E | D |
| | | M | I | L | D | | F | U | R | S | | | | |
| H | E | M | P | E | N | | T | I | N | Y | T | R | E | E |
| E | T | U | I | | E | X | U | L | T | | R | U | N | G |
| A | N | O | N | | S | I | R | E | S | | U | N | D | O |
| R | A | N | G | | S | I | F | T | | | M | E | S | S |

**Solution:**

| G | A | L | A | | | M | E | S | A | | O | D | O | R |
| A | R | E | S | | L | I | L | A | C | | V | I | V | A |
| S | E | E | P | | A | D | A | G | E | | E | V | E | N |
| P | A | K | I | S | T | A | N | | T | Y | R | A | N | T |
| | | | R | O | T | S | | N | O | E | L | | | |
| D | O | C | I | L | E | | S | E | N | S | A | T | E | |
| U | P | O | N | | R | A | M | I | E | | Y | O | L | K |
| C | I | A | | | K | E | G | | | | T | E | N | |
| T | U | T | U | | D | E | L | H | I | | F | A | C | E |
| | M | I | N | A | R | E | T | | S | V | E | L | T | E |
| | | | G | R | A | M | | A | R | I | A | | | |
| K | A | B | U | K | I | | T | E | A | M | S | T | E | R |
| I | S | L | E | | N | O | O | S | E | | T | A | R | O |
| L | I | E | N | | E | N | R | O | L | | E | X | I | T |
| T | A | U | T | | D | E | E | P | | | D | I | C | E |

**Solution:**

| W | R | A | P |  |  | E | T | U | I |  | C | E | D | E |
|---|---|---|---|---|---|---|---|---|---|---|---|---|---|---|
| H | A | L | O |  | V | I | A | N | D |  | R | E | E | L |
| A | G | E | S |  | I | G | L | O | O |  | A | L | M | S |
| M | U | S | T | A | C | H | E |  | L | A | S | S | I | E |
|  |  | M | I | T | T |  | L | I | D | S |  |  |  |  |
| F | E | R | A | R | I |  | G | U | Z | Z | L | E | S |  |
| A | G | I | N |  | M | I | N | C | E |  | Y | A | M | S |
| I | R | S |  |  | C | A | R |  |  | T | I | C |  |  |
| N | E | E | D |  | A | I | R | E | D |  | F | E | T | A |
|  | T | R | A | M | M | E | L |  | E | A | R | N | E | R |
|  |  |  | H | A | I | R |  | W | A | K | E |  |  |  |
| C | H | R | O | M | A |  | T | H | R | A | S | H | E | S |
| R | O | O | M |  | B | R | O | I | L |  | H | A | R | P |
| O | B | O | E |  | L | O | R | R | Y |  | E | Z | R | A |
| P | O | K | Y |  | E | W | E | R |  |  | N | E | S | T |

**Solution:**

| R | S | V | P |   |   | S | O | D | S |   | F | L | A | W |
| O | H | I | O |   | K | H | A | K | I |   | O | U | C | H |
| B | O | L | O |   | N | O | T | R | E |   | O | K | R | A |
| S | P | A | R | R | O | W | S |   | R | E | D | E | E | M |
|   |   |   |   | B | A | B | Y |   | B | R | O | W |   |   |
| E | N | T | O | M | B |   | E | R | A | S | E | R | S |   |
| N | A | R | Y |   | Y | A | X | I | S |   | B | A | L | D |
| D | I | E |   |   |   | R | I | B |   |   | Z | O | O |   |
| S | L | A | T |   | D | E | T | E | R |   | D | O | P | E |
|   | S | T | R | A | I | N | S |   | H | E | A | R | E | R |
|   |   | U | R | S | A |   | G | I | R | L |   |   |   |   |
| A | L | S | A | C | E |   | P | A | N | E | L | I | S | T |
| L | I | E | N |   | A | D | O | B | O |   | I | N | T | O |
| O | P | E | C |   | S | E | L | L | S |   | E | C | O | N |
| E | S | P | Y |   | E | L | L | E |   |   | R | A | P | S |

**Solution:**

| G | R | A | F |   |   | A | B | E | T |   | C | A | L | F |
|---|---|---|---|---|---|---|---|---|---|---|---|---|---|---|
| N | A | S | A |   | S | A | I | T | H |   | O | D | O | R |
| U | S | E | R |   | T | R | A | C | Y |   | N | A | P | E |
| S | H | A | M | P | O | O | S |   | R | O | A | R | E | D |
|   |   |   | C | O | I | N |   | S | O | A | K |   |   |   |
| M | O | S | A | I | C |   | S | T | I | R | R | E | D |   |
| E | M | I | T |   | S | W | O | R | D |   | Y | E | A | R |
| S | E | T |   |   |   | I | R | E |   |   |   | R | U | E |
| A | G | E | S |   | A | D | E | P | T |   | B | I | N | D |
|   | A | S | U | N | D | E | R |   | H | E | R | E | T | O |
|   | B | O | R | N |   | H | O | H | O |   |   |   |   |   |
| A | L | L | U | R | E |   | P | E | R | F | U | M | E | S |
| S | O | A | R |   | N | O | L | A | N |   | G | A | L | E |
| S | N | O | B |   | A | L | A | R | Y |   | H | U | L | A |
| N | E | S | S |   | L | E | T | S |   |   | T | I | E | S |

**Solution:**

| | | | | | | | | | | | | | | |
|---|---|---|---|---|---|---|---|---|---|---|---|---|---|---|
| S | T | A | G | # | # | O | I | N | K | # | D | A | D | S |
| T | R | U | E | # | S | P | O | O | L | # | E | V | E | N |
| A | I | N | T | # | M | E | T | R | E | # | C | O | M | A |
| B | O | T | S | W | A | N | A | # | E | A | R | W | I | G |
| # | # | # | W | A | C | S | # | E | N | V | Y | # | # | # |
| B | E | D | E | C | K | # | S | L | E | E | P | E | R | # |
| E | X | I | T | # | S | I | O | U | X | # | T | A | I | L |
| E | X | T | # | # | # | O | L | D | # | # | # | T | O | O |
| T | O | T | O | # | S | T | I | E | S | # | L | E | T | S |
| # | N | O | T | E | P | A | D | # | A | V | E | R | S | E |
| # | # | # | T | A | R | S | # | F | L | E | A | # | # | # |
| A | S | H | O | R | E | # | F | O | O | T | F | A | L | L |
| M | A | I | M | # | A | C | O | R | N | # | A | R | I | A |
| O | K | R | A | # | D | I | N | G | S | # | G | A | M | Y |
| S | E | E | N | # | S | A | T | E | # | # | E | B | B | S |

**Solution:**

| A | B | B | A | ■ |   | G | R | A | F | ■ | S | A | P | S |
| L | A | R | D | ■ | S | H | A | L | L | ■ | O | R | A | L |
| P | R | I | M | ■ | M | A | F | I | A | ■ | N | I | L | E |
| O | B | E | I | S | A | N | T | ■ | R | O | N | A | L | D |
| ■ |   |   | R | I | C | A | ■ | L | I | N | E | ■ |   |   |
| U | N | M | A | S | K | ■ | G | E | N | E | T | I | C |   |
| S | O | I | L |   | S | T | A | G | G | ■ | S | M | U | G |
| F | D | A | ■ |   | A | U | G | ■ |   | ■ | B | R | A |   |
| L | A | M | A |   | A | N | G | S | T |   | S | U | E | Z |
| ■ | L | I | C | E | N | S | E | ■ | I | M | P | E | D | E |
|   |   | T | O | N | Y | ■ | V | E | A | L | ■ |   |   |   |
| A | T | T | U | N | E | ■ | T | O | R | T | O | I | S | E |
| L | I | R | A | ■ | X | E | R | I | C | ■ | T | S | A | R |
| P | L | A | T | ■ | E | R | O | D | E | ■ | C | L | A | M |
| S | T | Y | E | ■ | D | R | Y | S | ■ | H | E | R | A |   |

**Solution:**

| S | P | A | S | | | S | T | I | R | | U | P | O | N |
|---|---|---|---|---|---|---|---|---|---|---|---|---|---|---|
| W | O | R | M | | B | A | Y | O | U | | N | E | B | E |
| A | S | E | A | | I | N | P | U | T | | H | A | I | R |
| P | H | A | R | I | S | E | E | | T | A | I | L | E | D |
| | T | I | E | R | | L | I | L | T | | | | | |
| C | Y | C | L | I | C | | C | Y | N | I | C | A | L | |
| O | O | Z | Y | | T | W | A | N | G | | H | A | L | O |
| D | U | E | | | I | N | C | | | | R | A | P | |
| A | R | C | H | | A | L | O | H | A | | C | O | M | A |
| | S | H | A | R | P | E | N | | V | E | R | N | A | L |
| | G | Y | P | S | | F | A | R | O | | | | | |
| C | U | D | G | E | L | | A | L | T | R | U | I | S | M |
| O | R | A | L | | A | P | N | E | A | | T | O | T | O |
| O | G | L | E | | U | T | T | E | R | | O | W | E | D |
| N | E | E | D | | D | A | I | S | | | N | A | M | E |

**Solution:**

| W | I | M | P | | | | I | O | T | A | | B | E | T | A |
|---|---|---|---|---|---|---|---|---|---|---|---|---|---|---|---|
| I | D | O | L | | | S | T | R | A | W | | I | R | A | N |
| S | E | R | E | | | C | A | B | I | N | | K | I | L | T |
| H | A | N | D | F | U | L | S | | I | C | I | C | L | E | |
| | | | G | A | R | Y | | A | N | O | N | | | | |
| M | E | T | E | O | R | | O | N | G | O | I | N | G | | |
| O | R | E | S | | Y | A | R | D | S | | S | U | R | E | |
| O | R | E | | | P | A | R | | | | R | O | T | | |
| T | O | T | E | | W | A | L | E | S | | A | S | S | N | |
| | R | H | U | B | A | R | B | | T | E | R | E | S | A | |
| | P | E | L | T | | F | U | S | S | | | | | | |
| P | E | A | H | E | N | | T | E | M | P | E | R | E | D | |
| U | M | B | O | | U | S | U | R | P | | N | I | C | E | |
| M | I | E | N | | T | E | R | M | S | | I | C | O | N | |
| A | R | T | Y | | S | A | K | I | | | C | A | N | T | |

**Solution:**

| F | I | S | H | ■ | ■ | A | B | C | S | ■ | T | H | E | N |
|---|---|---|---|---|---|---|---|---|---|---|---|---|---|---|
| I | O | T | A | ■ | S | T | O | N | Y | ■ | A | E | R | O |
| S | W | A | N | ■ | T | R | U | S | S | ■ | V | A | I | N |
| C | A | R | D | S | U | I | T | ■ | T | I | E | R | C | E |
| ■ | ■ | ■ | C | A | M | P | ■ | W | E | I | R | ■ | ■ | ■ |
| E | N | C | A | M | P | ■ | F | A | M | I | N | E | S | ■ |
| L | E | E | R | ■ | S | A | L | T | S | ■ | S | I | L | T |
| S | P | A | ■ | ■ | L | E | E | ■ | ■ | D | I | R |
| E | A | S | T | ■ | P | I | E | R | S | ■ | R | E | D | O |
| ■ | L | E | S | I | O | N | S | ■ | L | E | E | R | E | D |
| ■ | ■ | U | R | G | E | ■ | H | E | E | D | ■ | ■ | ■ |
| M | O | A | N | E | R | ■ | F | E | I | G | N | I | N | G |
| A | B | B | A | ■ | O | R | A | N | G | ■ | E | R | I | E |
| T | E | E | M | ■ | M | Y | R | R | H | ■ | C | O | N | N |
| S | Y | L | I | ■ | S | E | M | I | ■ | K | N | E | E |

**Solution:**

| S | T | U | B | | | B | O | S | C | | B | O | N | E |
|---|---|---|---|---|---|---|---|---|---|---|---|---|---|---|
| N | O | N | O | | H | A | I | K | U | | O | P | A | L |
| A | U | T | O | | A | D | L | I | B | | V | E | I | L |
| P | R | O | L | O | N | G | S | | I | C | I | C | L | E |
| | | | E | L | S | E | | I | C | O | N | | | |
| M | I | K | A | D | O | | I | L | L | N | E | S | S | |
| E | D | E | N | | M | O | V | I | E | | S | E | L | F |
| W | I | N | | | | V | I | A | | | | G | E | L |
| S | O | Y | A | | R | E | E | D | Y | | R | O | D | E |
| | T | A | L | K | E | R | S | | O | D | E | S | S | A |
| | | | K | I | S | S | | H | U | E | D | | | |
| A | S | K | A | N | T | | H | I | T | C | H | I | N | G |
| M | E | A | L | | F | O | U | R | H | | O | D | O | R |
| M | A | L | I | | U | R | G | E | S | | T | O | T | E |
| O | R | E | S | | L | E | E | S | | | S | L | E | W |

**Solution:**

| S | T | U | B | | | S | A | R | I | | H | O | G | S |
|---|---|---|---|---|---|---|---|---|---|---|---|---|---|---|
| E | A | R | L | | S | T | R | U | M | | A | L | O | E |
| A | L | S | O | | P | R | I | M | P | | L | E | A | N |
| M | E | A | S | U | R | E | D | | E | N | F | O | L | D |
| | | | S | N | I | P | | D | R | E | W | | | |
| U | P | R | O | O | T | | B | R | I | T | A | I | N | |
| S | L | A | M | | E | N | R | O | L | | Y | O | U | R |
| D | A | D | | | | E | E | L | | | | T | R | Y |
| A | S | I | A | | O | V | A | L | S | | N | A | S | A |
| | M | I | D | W | E | E | K | | A | R | I | S | E | N |
| | | | | H | E | R | R | | B | R | A | T | | |
| R | I | V | E | T | S | | P | R | O | G | R | A | M | S |
| O | D | O | R | | T | R | A | I | N | | O | R | A | L |
| D | O | T | E | | E | Y | I | N | G | | U | C | L | A |
| S | L | E | D | | D | E | N | Y | | | S | H | I | P |

**Solution:**

| E | A | C | H | | | F | A | L | A | | M | E | T | S |
|---|---|---|---|---|---|---|---|---|---|---|---|---|---|---|
| R | U | L | E | | B | O | S | O | M | | E | P | E | E |
| I | R | O | N | | A | L | I | G | N | | N | I | C | E |
| C | A | P | P | E | L | L | A | | E | P | O | C | H | S |
| | | | | E | A | S | Y | | T | S | A | R | | |
| S | A | N | C | T | A | | C | A | I | M | A | N | S | |
| T | R | E | K | | M | A | L | T | A | | H | A | I | R |
| E | R | A | | | | T | A | T | | | | I | R | E |
| P | O | T | S | | T | O | N | Y | S | | E | V | E | N |
| | W | H | A | L | I | N | G | | A | R | G | E | N | T |
| | | G | A | T | E | | C | L | E | G | | | | |
| A | L | A | U | D | A | | G | R | I | D | D | L | E | S |
| S | A | G | A | | N | O | L | A | N | | I | O | W | A |
| S | T | A | R | | I | N | A | N | E | | S | P | E | W |
| N | E | R | O | | C | E | D | E | | | H | E | R | S |

**Solution:**

| A | L | P | O | █ | █ | B | E | S | T | █ | L | A | C | K |
|---|---|---|---|---|---|---|---|---|---|---|---|---|---|---|
| L | I | E | D | █ | S | I | S | S | Y | █ | A | C | H | E |
| A | F | R | O | █ | T | A | P | E | R | █ | C | L | U | E |
| S | T | U | R | D | I | L | Y | █ | A | U | T | U | M | N |
| █ | █ | █ | O | I | L | Y | █ | O | N | T | O | █ | █ | █ |
| O | B | T | U | S | E | █ | P | I | N | E | S | O | L | █ |
| D | E | U | S | █ | S | C | A | L | Y | █ | E | R | I | C |
| O | F | T | █ | █ | █ | L | E | E | █ | █ | █ | G | N | U |
| R | O | O | M | █ | F | E | A | R | S | █ | P | A | D | S |
| █ | G | R | E | C | I | A | N | █ | H | A | U | N | T | S |
| █ | █ | T | E | N | T | █ | T | E | X | T | █ | █ | █ | █ |
| P | A | T | R | O | L | █ | D | U | K | E | D | O | M | S |
| E | T | U | I | █ | A | D | O | B | E | █ | O | B | O | E |
| R | O | T | C | █ | N | A | V | A | L | █ | W | I | R | E |
| O | P | U | S | █ | D | Y | E | S | █ | █ | N | E | E | D |

**Solution:**

| B | A | R | B | | | | E | C | H | O | | | S | W | A | P |
|---|---|---|---|---|---|---|---|---|---|---|---|---|---|---|---|---|
| A | R | E | A | | | B | E | A | U | X | | | T | A | X | I |
| L | I | A | R | | | B | R | I | E | F | | | E | V | E | N |
| L | A | M | B | S | K | I | N | | | O | G | R | E | S | S | |
| | | | | E | R | I | E | | | T | R | E | E | | | |
| S | T | A | L | I | N | | | H | I | D | E | O | U | S | | |
| H | A | U | L | | | G | O | A | T | S | | | S | L | A | Y |
| O | L | D | | | | | M | I | L | | | | C | U | E | |
| W | E | I | R | | | E | A | R | E | D | | | B | E | T | A |
| | S | T | A | R | C | H | Y | | | W | E | A | R | E | R | |
| | | | N | A | S | A | | | B | E | E | P | | | | |
| T | E | N | A | N | T | | | T | E | L | L | T | A | L | E | |
| S | T | O | W | | | A | T | O | L | L | | | I | C | E | D |
| A | U | R | A | | | S | E | L | L | S | | | Z | I | N | G |
| R | I | M | Y | | | Y | A | L | E | | | | E | D | D | Y |

**Solution:**

| T | S | A | R | | | M | A | G | I | | | S | N | O | W |
|---|---|---|---|---|---|---|---|---|---|---|---|---|---|---|---|
| O | K | R | A | | F | E | W | E | R | | | Y | O | G | A |
| F | I | E | F | | E | D | E | M | A | | | M | E | L | D |
| U | N | A | F | R | A | I | D | | N | A | P | L | E | S |   |
| | | | | L | I | R | A | | A | I | D | T | | | |
| S | C | H | E | M | E | | C | L | A | M | O | R | S | | |
| L | A | U | D | | D | R | A | I | N | | M | A | M | A | |
| E | L | L | | | | O | R | E | | | | D | E | L | |
| W | I | L | T | | T | B | O | N | E | | C | I | A | O | |
| | F | O | O | D | W | E | B | | R | E | H | I | R | E | |
| | | W | O | O | S | | U | R | S | A | | | | | |
| I | T | C | H | E | S | | I | S | O | T | O | P | E | S | |
| T | H | E | E | | O | R | D | E | R | | T | E | L | L | |
| C | O | D | A | | M | O | O | R | S | | I | S | L | E | |
| H | U | E | D | | E | E | L | S | | | C | O | E | D | |

**Solution:**

| T | S | A | R | | | M | A | G | I | | | S | N | O | W |
|---|---|---|---|---|---|---|---|---|---|---|---|---|---|---|---|
| O | K | R | A | | | F | E | W | E | R | | | Y | O | G | A |
| F | I | E | F | | | E | D | E | M | A | | | M | E | L | D |
| U | N | A | F | R | A | I | D | | | N | A | P | L | E | S |
| | | | | L | I | R | A | | | A | I | D | T | | |
| S | C | H | E | M | E | | | C | L | A | M | O | R | S | |
| L | A | U | D | | | D | R | A | I | N | | | M | A | M | A |
| E | L | L | | | | O | R | E | | | | | | D | E | L |
| W | I | L | T | | | T | B | O | N | E | | | C | I | A | O |
| | F | O | O | D | W | E | B | | | R | E | H | I | R | E |
| | | | W | O | O | S | | | U | R | S | A | | | |
| I | T | C | H | E | S | | | I | S | O | T | O | P | E | S |
| T | H | E | E | | | O | R | D | E | R | | | T | E | L | L |
| C | O | D | A | | | M | O | O | R | S | | | I | S | L | E |
| H | U | E | D | | | E | E | L | S | | | | C | O | E | D |

**Solution:**

| D | E | M | E | | | A | B | C | S | | A | M | M | O |
| E | V | I | L | | A | D | O | P | T | | L | O | A | M |
| M | E | S | A | | F | L | O | U | R | | I | N | C | A |
| I | N | S | P | I | R | I | T | | A | W | A | K | E | N |
| | | S | C | A | B | | R | I | B | S | | | | |
| R | E | D | E | E | M | | S | O | N | N | E | T | S | |
| U | S | E | D | | E | P | I | C | S | | S | A | L | T |
| S | T | M | | | I | N | K | | | | C | O | O | |
| H | E | I | R | | C | L | A | Y | S | | P | I | T | T |
| | S | T | I | M | U | L | I | | C | L | O | T | H | S |
| | | | P | A | S | S | | T | O | I | L | | | |
| A | S | P | E | C | T | | S | E | T | B | A | C | K | S |
| C | A | I | N | | A | B | O | R | T | | R | E | I | N |
| T | R | E | E | | R | O | O | M | Y | | I | N | T | O |
| G | I | R | D | | D | O | T | S | | | S | T | E | W |

**Solution:**

| C | R | O | W | ■ | ■ | A | R | T | S | ■ | W | A | S | H |
|---|---|---|---|---|---|---|---|---|---|---|---|---|---|---|
| H | U | G | H | ■ | F | L | O | U | T | ■ | I | N | C | A |
| I | S | L | E | ■ | E | L | D | E | R | ■ | R | O | A | M |
| C | H | E | E | R | I | O | S | ■ | A | G | E | N | T | S |
| ■ | ■ | ■ | D | I | N | T | ■ | T | I | N | T | ■ | ■ | ■ |
| S | C | U | L | P | T | ■ | H | O | T | P | A | D | S | ■ |
| C | A | S | E | ■ | S | C | A | R | S | ■ | P | E | T | E |
| O | R | E | ■ | ■ | ■ | H | I | T | ■ | ■ | ■ | L | E | D |
| T | E | R | M | ■ | P | A | T | S | Y | ■ | C | H | A | D |
| ■ | T | S | U | N | A | M | I | ■ | A | I | R | I | L | Y |
| ■ | ■ | S | N | I | P | ■ | O | N | C | E | ■ | ■ | ■ | ■ |
| H | I | T | T | E | R | ■ | M | A | K | E | S | M | A | D |
| O | O | Z | E | ■ | I | R | A | T | E | ■ | T | I | K | I |
| S | T | A | R | ■ | N | I | C | H | E | ■ | E | M | I | R |
| P | A | R | S | ■ | G | O | E | S | ■ | ■ | D | E | N | T |

**Solution:**

| A | T | O | P |   |   | F | L | A | N |   | R | S | V | P |
|---|---|---|---|---|---|---|---|---|---|---|---|---|---|---|
| S | E | G | O |   | R | A | I | S | E |   | E | W | E | R |
| E | E | L | S |   | H | U | L | L | S |   | F | I | R | E |
| A | M | E | T | H | Y | S | T |   | T | H | U | M | B | S |
|   |   |   | M | I | T | T |   | G | L | E | N |   |   |   |
| J | O | S | E | P | H |   | S | L | E | N | D | E | R |   |
| O | P | E | N |   | M | A | T | E | D |   | S | T | O | P |
| S | I | N |   |   | Z | E | N |   |   |   | H | A | T |   |
| E | N | D | S |   | S | T | A | S | H |   | P | I | C | A |
|   | E | S | C | A | P | E | D |   | E | P | O | C | H | S |
|   |   | E | R | I | C |   | C | A | S | E |   |   |   |   |
| D | A | M | P | E | N |   | L | A | T | I | T | U | D | E |
| R | I | O | T |   | A | F | I | R | E |   | I | C | E | D |
| I | D | L | E |   | C | L | E | A | R |   | C | L | E | G |
| P | E | E | R |   | H | U | N | T |   |   | S | A | M | E |

**Solution:**

```
H A R D █ N I B S █ F L I T
A V O W █ P E R O T █ R E D O
L I M A █ S P I N Y █ O S L O
O V E R S E A S █ L I N T E L
█ F O U L █ S I L T █
O F F E N D █ E N S L A V E
B O L D █ O N I O N █ L A V E
O L E █ A D O █ L A Y
E D E N █ P I E T Y █ F I D E
█ S T E L L A R █ E R O D E D
█ B E A D █ B L U R █
T E L U G U █ T E L E G R A M
O R A L █ D I R G E █ E U R O
P I T A █ I C I E R █ T S A R
S E E R █ T E X T █ S E B E
```

**Solution:**

| S | W | A | P | | | A | P | E | D | | W | H | E | T |
|---|---|---|---|---|---|---|---|---|---|---|---|---|---|---|
| A | I | D | E | | A | C | H | O | O | | E | U | R | O |
| S | T | A | G | | W | H | I | S | T | | A | R | I | A |
| S | H | R | A | P | N | E | L | | T | I | L | L | E | D |
| | S | A | I | D | | T | I | N | T | | | | | |
| C | O | L | U | M | N | | P | U | N | C | H | E | D | |
| A | M | O | S | | G | O | I | N | G | | Y | E | A | R |
| R | A | G | | | P | E | A | | | R | I | O | | |
| S | H | O | T | U | R | T | S | Y | | S | I | L | T | |
| | A | S | H | T | R | A | Y | | A | L | L | E | Y | S |
| | R | I | C | H | | K | N | E | E | | | | | |
| G | R | O | U | C | H | | L | I | K | E | N | E | S | S |
| R | O | W | S | | I | R | A | T | E | | D | R | E | W |
| A | B | E | T | | N | A | M | E | D | | E | M | M | A |
| B | E | D | S | | S | W | B | S | | | R | A | I | N |

**Solution:**

| S | W | A | P | ■ | A | P | E | D | ■ | W | H | E | T |
|---|---|---|---|---|---|---|---|---|---|---|---|---|---|
| A | I | D | E | ■ | A | C | H | O | O | ■ | E | U | R | O |
| S | T | A | G | ■ | W | H | I | S | T | ■ | A | R | I | A |
| S | H | R | A | P | N | E | L | ■ | T | I | L | L | E | D |
| ■ | S | A | I | D | ■ | T | I | N | T | ■ |
| C | O | L | U | M | N | ■ | P | U | N | C | H | E | D | ■ |
| A | M | O | S | ■ | G | O | I | N | G | ■ | Y | E | A | R |
| R | A | G | ■ | P | E | A | ■ | R | I | O |
| S | H | O | T | U | R | T | S | Y | ■ | S | I | L | T |
| ■ | A | S | H | T | R | A | Y | ■ | A | L | L | E | Y | S |
| R | I | C | H | ■ | K | N | E | E | ■ |
| G | R | O | U | C | H | L | I | K | E | N | E | S | S |
| R | O | W | S | ■ | I | R | A | T | E | ■ | D | R | E | W |
| A | B | E | T | ■ | N | A | M | E | D | ■ | E | M | M | A |
| B | E | D | S | ■ | S | W | B | S | ■ | R | A | I | N |

**Solution:**

| S | E | B | E | ■ | ■ | D | A | L | E | ■ | P | R | E | P |
|---|---|---|---|---|---|---|---|---|---|---|---|---|---|---|
| W | R | A | P | ■ | S | A | T | Y | R | ■ | I | O | W | A |
| A | I | R | S | ■ | O | T | T | E | R | ■ | S | T | E | W |
| M | C | K | I | N | L | E | Y | ■ | A | L | T | E | R | S |
| ■ | ■ | ■ | L | O | I | S | ■ | O | N | T | O | ■ | ■ | ■ |
| S | E | C | O | N | D | ■ | F | U | D | D | L | E | D | ■ |
| A | N | O | N | ■ | S | L | A | T | S | ■ | S | L | O | B |
| U | N | O | ■ | ■ | I | R | E | ■ | ■ | O | R | E | | |
| L | U | K | E | ■ | I | N | E | R | T | ■ | A | P | I | A |
| ■ | I | S | L | A | N | D | S | ■ | E | F | F | E | C | T |
| ■ | A | R | E | A | ■ | D | E | M | E | ■ | | | | |
| E | M | O | T | E | R | ■ | B | U | N | G | A | L | O | W |
| B | A | L | I | ■ | T | E | A | M | S | ■ | R | O | P | E |
| O | R | E | O | ■ | I | N | L | A | Y | ■ | E | P | E | E |
| N | E | O | N | ■ | A | D | D | S | ■ | D | E | C | K | |

**Solution:**

| A | C | T | H |  |  | A | F | E | W |  | S | H | E | D |
| S | H | O | O |  | A | L | L | A | H |  | H | A | L | E |
| E | A | R | L |  | C | A | I | R | O |  | R | U | L | E |
| A | R | T | I | F | A | C | T |  | R | A | I | L | E | D |
|  |  |  | D | O | C | K |  | E | L | S | E |  |  |  |
| S | A | F | A | R | I |  | T | R | E | K | K | E | D |  |
| A | L | L | Y |  | A | I | R | E | D |  | S | N | O | W |
| T | A | I |  |  | N | Y | C |  |  |  | R | Y | E |  |
| E | T | N | A |  | L | U | S | T | S |  | P | O | L | L |
|  | E | G | G | P | A | R | T |  | P | O | O | L | E | D |
|  |  | R | O | S | E |  | S | O | P | S |  |  |  |  |
| D | A | K | O | T | A |  | S | C | O | T | S | M | A | N |
| A | C | L | U |  | G | R | A | I | N |  | E | A | S | E |
| I | R | A | N |  | N | O | N | O | S |  | S | K | I | S |
| S | E | N | D |  | E | D | E | N |  |  | S | E | A | S |

**Solution:**

| B | L | O | B |   |   | S | E | B | S |   | F | L | E | A |
|---|---|---|---|---|---|---|---|---|---|---|---|---|---|---|
| L | I | M | A |   | A | P | P | A | L |   | L | I | A | R |
| V | E | E | R |   | T | E | E | N | Y |   | A | P | S | E |
| D | U | N | G | A | R | E | E |   | N | A | U | S | E | A |
|   |   |   | A | V | I | D |   | S | E | P | T |   |   |   |
| M | I | L | I | E | U |   | E | C | S | T | A | S | Y |   |
| I | R | A | N |   | M | E | M | O | S |   | S | C | O | T |
| N | I | X |   |   |   | M | O | W |   |   |   | O | U | R |
| I | S | L | E |   | W | E | T | L | Y |   | D | U | N | E |
|   | H | Y | G | I | E | N | E |   | E | M | E | R | G | E |
|   |   | G | R | A | D |   | F | O | O | L |   |   |   |   |
| S | C | O | R | E | R |   | S | A | M | O | V | A | R | S |
| T | A | R | O |   | O | P | E | R | A |   | I | D | O | L |
| O | P | A | L |   | U | R | B | A | N |   | N | A | T | O |
| W | E | L | L |   | T | O | E | D |   |   | G | R | E | W |

**Solution:**

| S | K | I | P |   |   | S | A | R | I |   |   | P | E | S | T |
|---|---|---|---|---|---|---|---|---|---|---|---|---|---|---|---|
| W | E | R | E |   |   | P | I | C | O | T |   | I | D | E | A |
| B | R | A | N |   |   | A | Z | T | E | C |   | G | I | R | L |
| W | I | N | N | I | P | E | G |   |   | H | O | S | T | E | L |
|   |   |   | A | C | A | D |   |   | H | I | C | K |   |   |   |
| P | H | O | N | E | Y |   |   | P | O | N | T | I | A | C |   |
| L | O | S | T |   |   | A | M | O | N | G |   |   | N | U | L | L |
| A | H | A |   |   |   | I | R | K |   |   |   |   | D | I | E |
| Y | O | K | E |   |   | F | L | E | S | H |   | L | I | M | A |
|   | S | A | M | P | L | E | D |   |   | O | R | A | T | E | D |
|   |   |   | P | L | U | S |   |   | I | M | P | S |   |   |   |
| E | S | S | A | Y | S |   |   | A | N | I | M | A | T | E | S |
| M | E | E | T |   |   | H | O | G | A | N |   |   | G | A | L | E |
| M | A | C | H |   |   | E | B | O | N | Y |   | N | I | L | E |
| A | R | T | Y |   |   | S | I | N | E |   |   | A | L | E | S |

**Solution:**

| S | K | I | P |   |   | S | A | R | I |   | P | E | S | T |
|---|---|---|---|---|---|---|---|---|---|---|---|---|---|---|
| W | E | R | E |   | P | I | C | O | T |   | I | D | E | A |
| B | R | A | N |   | A | Z | T | E | C |   | G | I | R | L |
| W | I | N | N | I | P | E | G |   | H | O | S | T | E | L |
|   |   |   | A | C | A | D |   | H | I | C | K |   |   |   |
| P | H | O | N | E | Y |   | P | O | N | T | I | A | C |   |
| L | O | S | T |   | A | M | O | N | G |   | N | U | L | L |
| A | H | A |   |   | I | R | K |   |   |   | D | I | E |   |
| Y | O | K | E |   | F | L | E | S | H |   | L | I | M | A |
|   | S | A | M | P | L | E | D |   | O | R | A | T | E | D |
|   |   | P | L | U | S |   | I | M | P | S |   |   |   |   |
| E | S | S | A | Y | S |   | A | N | I | M | A | T | E | S |
| M | E | E | T |   | H | O | G | A | N |   | G | A | L | E |
| M | A | C | H |   | E | B | O | N | Y |   | N | I | L | E |
| A | R | T | Y |   | S | I | N | E |   |   | A | L | E | S |

**Solution:**

| H | A | W | K | | | S | U | D | S | | | E | L | S | E |
|---|---|---|---|---|---|---|---|---|---|---|---|---|---|---|---|
| O | H | I | O | | A | P | N | E | A | | | R | I | L | L |
| P | E | S | O | | C | O | I | N | S | | | O | R | A | L |
| I | M | P | L | I | C | I | T | | S | E | S | A | M | E | |
| | | | A | B | E | L | | T | I | K | I | | | | |
| C | L | A | I | M | S | | N | I | N | E | V | E | H | | |
| Y | A | R | D | | S | T | A | G | G | | E | M | I | T | |
| S | T | Y | | | | A | S | H | | | | B | R | A | |
| T | H | A | I | | W | R | A | T | H | | B | E | E | P | |
| | E | N | S | N | A | R | L | | A | W | A | R | D | S | |
| | | | O | N | L | Y | | E | V | I | L | | | | |
| P | O | L | L | E | N | | A | M | E | N | A | B | L | E | |
| A | R | E | A | | U | N | P | I | N | | | N | O | E | S |
| S | E | A | T | | T | O | I | L | S | | | C | L | A | P |
| T | O | N | E | | S | W | A | Y | | | | E | D | D | Y |

**Solution:**

| C | H | A | D | | | P | O | E | T | | B | L | E | W |
|---|---|---|---|---|---|---|---|---|---|---|---|---|---|---|
| L | U | G | E | | A | S | K | E | W | | Y | O | U | R |
| A | L | A | R | | C | A | R | L | O | | W | I | R | E |
| P | A | R | A | B | O | L | A | | S | E | A | S | O | N |
| | | | N | O | R | M | | M | O | B | Y | | | |
| S | L | O | G | A | N | | S | Y | M | B | O | L | S | |
| H | E | B | E | | S | H | A | L | E | | F | E | E | L |
| A | T | E | | | | A | K | A | | | | T | W | O |
| G | U | Y | S | | C | L | E | R | K | | A | G | E | S |
| | P | S | Y | C | H | O | S | | I | G | N | O | R | E |
| | | S | P | A | S | | S | T | A | G | | | | |
| F | E | S | T | A | L | | L | E | S | S | E | N | E | D |
| A | C | H | E | | I | S | A | A | C | | R | E | D | O |
| T | H | E | M | | C | O | U | T | H | | E | R | I | E |
| S | O | D | S | | E | N | D | S | | | D | O | T | S |

**Solution:**

| S | P | I | N | | | A | L | M | S | | | R | A | R | E |
|---|---|---|---|---|---|---|---|---|---|---|---|---|---|---|---|
| W | O | R | E | | W | H | I | S | K | | | E | M | I | R |
| B | L | A | B | | H | E | D | G | E | | | S | O | F | A |
| S | E | Q | U | O | I | A | S | | P | L | U | S | E | S | |
| | | | | L | A | N | D | | A | T | O | M | | | |
| S | T | R | A | F | E | | E | X | I | G | E | N | T | | |
| T | R | E | E | | R | E | L | I | C | | D | O | O | R | |
| Y | A | P | | | | N | B | A | | | | T | R | Y | |
| E | D | A | M | | D | R | O | L | L | | M | E | S | A | |
| | E | Y | E | B | R | O | W | | E | D | I | S | O | N | |
| | | | D | E | A | L | | A | V | I | S | | | | |
| D | O | G | L | E | G | | B | R | I | E | F | I | N | G | |
| I | S | L | E | | G | A | U | G | E | | | I | D | E | A |
| P | L | A | Y | | E | G | G | O | S | | | L | O | S | T |
| S | O | D | S | | R | E | S | T | | | | E | L | S | E |

Made in United States
North Haven, CT
05 May 2022

18895383R00102